MASTERING MOTHERHOOD

Books in the Woman's Workshop Series

Woman's Workshop Series

MASTERING MOTHERHOOD

BARBARA BUSH

ZondervanPublishingHouse

Grand Rapids, Michigan

A Division of HarperCollinsPublishers

For Stephen, David,
Gary, Patricia,
my treasure and my reward

CONTENTS

1

FIGHTING THE CURRENT

The waters along the California beaches can be dangerous and should always be treated with proper respect and caution. Even on calm days, when the green flags are out, the surf can be tricky. Cooling off in ankle-deep water, adults and children alike may be forced to employ some fancy footwork in order to keep their balance as the undertow of receding water sucks the sand from beneath their feet on its way seaward.

On days when especially hazardous conditions such as riptides prevail, lifeguards fly red flags to warn swimmers and surfers. A riptide is caused when water, pushed to shore by the oncoming surf, cannot flow out again. Since it is unable to break through the crashing waves behind it, the water flows laterally along the shoreline in a sort of river that can attain the width of two football fields, searching for a weak spot in the breakers that will enable it to make its way back out to sea.

A child playing in two feet of water can suddenly be swept away by this unpredictable river; and when the current finds an opening, he may be carried hundreds of yards seaward within a matter of minutes. Lifeguards at a single station often make over four hundred rescues per day under such conditions—rescues that include veteran as well as inexperienced swimmers.

Most women do not need to see red flags to know that many of the prevailing currents in today's society are dangerous to them. They feel personally threatened by some of the very programs and pronouncements that are supposed to improve their lives. Christian women, in particular, are alarmed over many of the statements made by women's groups, statements which run counter to their beliefs.

Gloria Steinem, in an interview in *Redbook* magazine, said, "Marriage itself, or marriage and the family, are now instruments of women's oppression. The institution is wrong, not the people in it."[1] As editor of *Ms.* magazine she said, "By the year 2000 we will, I hope, raise our children to believe in human potential, not God."[2]

The Humanist Manifesto II, signed by Betty Friedan, founder of National Organization for Women, states, "No deity will save us, we must save ourselves. Promises of immortal salvation are both illusory and harmful."[3]

Shirley MacLaine, actress and outspoken feminist, made it clear that she understands that her anti-family views are anti-Christian as well when she stated,

> The idea of the father being the head of the family . . . that he brings home the bacon while his wife brings up the children and sees to their physical needs—that is obsolete, no question about it. All this goes back as far as Christian culture, to what Mary and Joseph started. It's just a million things that have been handed down with the Christian ethic, so when you begin to question the family, you have to question all those things.
>
> I don't think it's desirable to conform to having one mate and for those two people to raise children. . . . This is not the natural behavior pattern of a human individual—people who behave that way are operating out of repressive culture, out of Christian doctrine, out of Thou Shalt Not Commit Adultery, in one of the Ten Commandments.[4]

Perhaps the most chilling assertion has been given to us by Dr. Mary Jo Bane, associate director of Wellesley College's Center for Research on Woman. She says, "We really don't know how to raise children. . . . The fact that children are raised in families means there's no equality. . . . In order to raise children with equality, we must take them away from families and raise them."[5]

Statements like these not only attack a woman's standing as wife, they also denigrate her status as a mother, a position once held universally in high esteem. The wholesale performance of abortions further erodes the status of motherhood: If the life of the fetus is of so little value, how important can the job of caring for those who are not aborted be in the eyes of society? Even the idea of zero population growth, carried to its logical conclusion, implies a negative attitude toward children and a rather grudging agreement to share our land and air with a limited number of them.

So the Christian mother finds herself in the center of controversy, attempting to sort out contradictory, disturbing messages and to come to a knowledge of the truth.

"You must not waste your potential by staying at home; such waste is sinful."

"Your children are the most important investment you can make."

"The man is the head of the home."

"Husband and wife must be completely equal."

"Any family with more than two children is a drain on society and on the earth's resources."

"We must strive for a simpler life style."

"A woman must be beautifully groomed and sexy at all times."

"Be yourself!"

"You are responsible for the kind of people your children become."

"Your child's personhood must not be violated."

These and many other themes leave mothers feeling as if the ground on which they are standing, on which generations of mothers have stood with confidence, is being sucked out from under them by the tide of popular opinion, and they find themselves scrambling desperately for safety. Some are being swept along by the current, carried relentlessly away from the security of familiar standards of behavior, carried out to sea at the mercy of whatever tides and winds prevail at the moment.

Actress-photographer-journalist Candace Bergen sounded a plaintive note in a lengthy, commendably honest interview in the *Los Angeles Times*. Among other things, she said,

There's a whole group of people my age—the atomic babies—who grew up with no faith in anything at all. We . . .

spent our teens and twenties disencumbering ourselves from traditional values, making ourselves what we thought was free. Now we realize that maybe what we've done is give up the things we really want most—the possibility to have children and a family life.

A few months ago I gave an interview to *Vogue* magazine and said, "It's all just beginning folks, this is the best time of life." But that's just total bull. An hour later I got so frightened I could barely speak or walk. I sat in my apartment for about six weeks dealing with all the conflicts women feel at this age. If you haven't had a husband and children, you start to deal intensely with the dilemma of whether you'll ever have them.

It was exhilarating for a while, to give up all those old traditional values, to feel that one didn't need to be completed by a man—that it was possible to have a life without children and not feel incomplete. But the feeling doesn't last.

So now I'm wondering if all this liberation shouldn't be reevaluated. I mean, five years ago I thought the most courageous thing was not to get married, not to have children. That all seemed so predictable and safe. Now I think the most courageous thing is to get married and *have* children, because that seems the most worthwhile, if not the most impossible, thing to try for. There are certain age-old realities you can't refute.[6]

Jesus had something to say about sand and safe ground. He said that those who did not act on His words were foolish, building their houses on sand that would not hold up to the wind and rain, and therefore be destroyed. The houses that would stand the storms of life—the houses of the wise—were those built on solid rock, the rock of hearing and doing His words (Matt. 7:24-27).

The Christian mother, then, must turn a deaf ear to the babble of voices vying for her attention and listen to God. It is in Scripture that she will find the only safe and reliable information about how to fulfill her calling as wife and mother.

Motherhood involves the acquiring of skills, the application of principles, and the expression of attitudes and emotions. In parts of the secular world, a person begins a trade as an apprentice. After a predetermined amount of skill is acquired, the apprentice is advanced to the level of journeyman; and eventually, if he is persistent and able, he reaches the status of master of his trade.

Even though they may reject attempts to downgrade the role of mother and accept the high value placed upon motherhood by God, many Christian women enter motherhood feeling as green and incompetent as any apprentice ever did. They feel that actually enjoying their children, relaxing and having fun with obedient, confident offspring may be possible for other, wiser women, but not for them. They have a scarcity of skills, scanty knowledge, and inconsistent attitudes and emotions.

But God does not intend for any child of His to remain at this beginning level. He gave us Scripture so that each of us "may be thoroughly equipped for every good work" (2 Tim. 3:16-17). The Bible has a great deal to say about exactly how to go about our tasks as parents and mothers. If we hear and do what God says, we will build a strong house on safe ground, just as Jesus promised we could. We will become, with God's strength, master mothers, equipped for every good work.

Making It Personal

1. How do you feel about the statements made by prominent women in this chapter? _____

_____

_____

_____

2. What trends in today's society bother you as a mother?

_____

_____

_____

3. Where does a Christian mother look for guidance when she is confused about what is right? (Read Matt. 7:24-27.)

_____

_____

_____

4. In what three areas must a mother grow? _____

_____

_____

_____

5. Can we pick and choose which parts of God's plan we will follow if we want to be successful? (Josh. 1:7-8; Matt. 5:17-19.) _____

_____

_____

_____

6. Where should parents get wisdom for rearing their children (Judg. 13:8, 13)? _____

_____

_____

Before you read on. . . . Do you feel anyone understands you? If so, who? / Do you feel that God has a purpose for you? If so, could you say what that purpose would be? / To whom can you turn when you are distressed? / How much does God know about you personally? / Read Psalm 139:13-16.

2

GOD'S RELATIONSHIP TO MOTHERS

A few years ago, a magazine advertisement caught my attention. "Who mothers mothers?" it asked. Those words so affected me that I still think about them from time to time, especially when life seems to be piling up. It is not enough to have people agree that mothering is an endless and demanding job. What every mother wants to know is, *Who cares when I am worn out? Who understands the pressures I feel? Where can I turn for help?*

God As Father

Few things in Scripture are taught as clearly as the fact that God wants His children to think of Him as their Father. God referred to Himself by that title several times in the Old Testament, but the message didn't seem to sink in. The Jews considered God more as a Father to the entire nation rather than part of the one-to-one relationship we find stressed in the New Testament.

If it were not for Jesus, we might feel it presumptuous to think of God as our personal Father. But Jesus repeatedly emphasized the Father-Child relationship available to those who came to God through Him, using seventeen such references in the Sermon on the Mount alone!

However, the Bible also makes it clear that *God is not our Father simply because we are human beings.* Only those who have received Jesus have been given the privilege of being children of God (John 1:12). *Only Christians have a right to call God "Father."*

This is important for mothers to understand, because they will be completely frustrated in their attempts to feel comforted by God and to be the kind of mothers He wants them to be if they are not really His children. Unless they are born again spiritually into His family they will have no power in their lives to do His will. They will be like Christmas trees with God's principles attached to the branches of their lives like glittering ornaments, rather than trees that blossom and produce true fruit because of the living power that flows through them.

If you have never become God's child, if you realize you

have never asked Jesus to be your personal Lord and Savior, why not stop and do it now? When you ask Jesus to dwell within you, He will forgive your past sins and failures and enable you to live a life pleasing to Him in every way, including your life as a mother. God will then truly be your own personal Father (Gal. 4:4-6)!

Motherhood: God's Idea

God wants to be our Father, but He also completely understands the role of mother—a role, let us remind ourselves, He created in the first place. Motherhood is God's idea. This simple fact sometimes escapes us. God created both male and female in His image (Gen. 1:27). Therefore, just like a human inventor, so the heavenly Father knows everything there is to know about His invention—the way it works, its intended use, its limitations, its proper care.

But God not only created mothers, He also identified Himself with them. In Isaiah 66:12-13, God promises, "You shall be nursed, you shall be carried on the hip and fondled on the knees. As one whom his mother comforts, so I will comfort you" (NASB). Jesus showed He also understood a mother's feelings when He declared that He wanted to gather the "children" Jews of Jerusalem to Himself as a mother hen gathers her chicks under her wings (Matt. 23:37).

But God goes beyond general knowledge about mothers, for the Bible assures us that each of us, personally, is understood by God. He knew about each of us before we were born, a truth that should both comfort us and give pause to those who favor abortions on demand. Psalm 139:13-16 informs us, "You created my inmost being; you knit me together in my mother's womb. I praise you because I am fearfully and wonderfully made . . . your eyes saw my unformed body. All the days ordained for me were written in your book before one of them came to be." God said to Jeremiah, "Before I formed you in the womb I knew you, before you were born I set you apart" (Jer. 1:5).

The age-old cry of the adolescent, "You don't understand!" often expresses the feelings of mothers as they turn to other human beings for solace. Husbands may not always be willing or able to meet our needs. Friends may have their own problems to deal with. Counselors may lack insight into our particular situations.

So who mothers mothers? God does. We can come confidently to Him in our time of need (Heb. 4:16), certain that He is not removed from our experiences as mothers. He created our world; He created man as male and female. The whole idea of sex, children, mothers, fathers, and families is His; and God also knows everything about each of us individually.

Our deep need to be assured that someone really understands us, to share our innermost feelings with another, is not silly. It is a yearning built into our natures by God at creation. Adam was surrounded by living creatures, but "for Adam no suitable helper was found" (Gen. 2:20). When Eve was created, Adam's reaction was, "This is now bone of my bone and flesh of my flesh" (2:23).

It is this sense of recognition, this desire to have a relationship with someone who is capable of understanding our unique predicament, that all people, including mothers, long for. The fact that God lived as a human being on this earth has personal meaning for each of us for this very reason. We rejoice as we remember that "we do not have a high priest who is unable to sympathize with our weaknesses, but we have one who has been tempted in every way, just as we are—yet was without sin" (Heb. 4:15).

Stamp collectors love to get together with other stamp collectors. They like to discuss perforations, watermarks, and overprints with others who comprehend their significance.

Gardeners enjoy comparing results with other plant lovers, and good cooks can't wait to pass on new recipes to others who share their interest. This basic need to experience things in common with others is part of our natures and brings us deep satisfaction.

I have often thought that one of the greatest burdens of the elderly may be that they are survivors of an age which no one can really share with them. They cannot relive old memories with anyone who was there, for many of their companions are dead. Those around them are comparative youngsters who think of them as "old Mrs. So-and-So," and who are unable to picture them as teen-agers, young mothers, or people with exciting events in their past.

Mothers, surrounded day after day by children who think of them only in that role, need the assurance that someone understands the rest of their personalities as well. They need to feel that there is a sympathetic ear available when the pressures of motherhood and of life in general build up. Thankfully, husbands and friends are part of God's plan for us, and our relationships with them restore our sagging spirits and increase our enjoyment of good times.

But human companionship is not always available when we need it, nor is human wisdom always sufficient for the trials of life. Our own resources are sometimes in short supply, especially as we try to meet the daily demands which rearing children places on them.

It is essential, then, for us to know that we are not on our own as mothers without a divine hand to guide or a source of wisdom to which to turn. The God who understands each of us completely as a person is also our everlasting Father and the Master of every skill needed for godly motherhood.

Making It Personal

1. How does God want us to think of Him? _____

_____

_____

_____

2. How does God become a person's Father? _____

_____

_____

_____

3. If you have never done so, is there any reason you should not ask God to become your personal father by receiving Jesus into your life right now? (John 14:6) _____

_____

_____

_____

4. On what three levels does God understand mothers?

_____

_____

_____

5. Why do we need to feel understood? _____

_____

_____

_____

6. Where can we turn when we feel no one understands?

_____

_____

Before you read on. . . . How would you describe your mother? / What kind of person was your father? / How do you feel about the way you were treated as a child? What was good and what was bad? / Have you thanked God and your parents for the good things?

Read Hebrews 12:15. Have you forgiven your parents for any injustices you feel you received from them? Read Ephesians 4:31-32. / Where did you get the ideas you have about what God is like?

3

WHAT KIND OF PARENT IS GOD?

Some of the churches my husband has pastored have had weekday preschools, and it has been his custom to take part often in their chapel services. It is a challenge for him to come up with something that is interesting enough to keep three-

and four-year-olds attentive for even a few minutes and that teaches them something as well. One morning he decided to put on the robe he wears for special occasions and explain to the youngsters, many of whom did not belong to church families, what goes on during a worship service. After his presentation, he returned to his office across the hallway from the sanctuary and continued his work.

A short time later he heard a child yelling in the hall and opened his door a crack to see what was going on. A little boy was pulling his mother down the corridor, shouting, "Hurry! Hurry! You might miss him!" When they reached the sanctuary door, the mother helped her son as he struggled to open it. Looking inside, the little boy's face fell. "Oh, no, he's gone!" he exclaimed. "Mother, you should have seen him. God was here this morning, and he was just beautiful!"

Many adults have no more accurate idea about what God is really like than this little boy had; and while it is understandable that a child should be confused, it is a tragedy when an adult is so misinformed.

Particularly in view of the fact that God wants to be a Father to His children, each of us must answer the question: What kind of parent do I think God is? Our response to that question will probably indicate the pattern, recognized or unrecognized, for our own actions as a parent. Jesus said, "Be perfect, therefore, as your heavenly Father is perfect" (Matt. 5:48). In order even to contemplate such a task, we had better be sure that our conclusions as to what a perfect God is like are correct.

Is God the Father aloof, detached, not really involved in the daily dreams and disappointments of His children? Is He vindictive, interested only in ferreting out every negative thought, word, and deed of each child, a frown of disapproval continually on His brow? Is He like some cosmic policeman, never commending positive actions, but bent only on catching anyone who steps over a legal line? Or do you think that our heavenly Father is like Santa Claus, always beaming and handing out candy, who may make a list and check it twice, but ends up giving identical gifts to both the naughty and nice? Is God the kind of person who can't tell anyone no? When we give Him our sweetest smiles does He turn all soft and gooey on the inside and let us have our way?

Any of the above views, lodged in the mind, will lead us into grave error as we try to live out our roles as godly parents. To be godly parents means, obviously, to be as Godlike as possible. How important it is, then, to examine carefully what kind of parent God approves of and what kind of Father God has revealed Himself to be! And the only place we can turn to find that out is the Bible.

One of the biggest problems encountered when reading the Bible is that we tend to be "wired" by our backgrounds to pick up certain verbal signals. In spoken or written communication, certain words or concepts jump out at us, while other words never get through our unconscious screening device at all. Those who think of God as having a forbidding nature pick up only the judgmental aspects of a passage, while those with a sentimental sort of God in mind can't grasp any truths except those having to do with love and peace.

If a woman conjures up visions of a wrathful being hurling thunderbolts from heaven every time she thinks of God, she should immerse her mind in passages of Scripture like the following until another image of God becomes real to her:

"Give thinks to the LORD, for he is good; his love endures forever" (Ps. 118:1).

". . . the Father himself loves you . . ." (John 16:27).

"Whoever does not love does not know God, because God is love. . . . This is love: not that we loved God, but that he loved us . . ." (1 John 4:8, 10).

"But God demonstrates his own love for us in this: While we were still sinners, Christ died for us" (Rom. 5:8).

For any who feel that the Lord is too loving to condemn anyone and is indulgent toward those who disobey Him, I would suggest a thorough perusal of the following passages:

"Consider therefore the kindness and sternness of God: sternness to those who fell, but kindness to you . . ." (Rom. 11:22).

"Because the Lord disciplines those he loves, and he punishes everyone he accepts as a son" (Heb. 12:6).

"The Son of Man will send out his angels, and they will weed out of his kingdom everything that causes sin and all who do evil. They will throw them into the fiery furnace, where there will be weeping and gnashing of teeth" (Matt. 13:41-42).

Our ideas about God are accumulated from many nonbiblical sources. The kind of person our own father was often enters the picture whenever we try to visualize our heavenly Father. Fairy stories from our childhood, myths about pagan Roman and Greek gods color our thinking. As Christians it is hard to judge to what extent our views are affected by the world and its influence. We may have left our pre-Christian notions of God unchallenged and continued to accept blindly the popular versions of "the man upstairs," or "somebody bigger than you and I." All these indicate some nebulous being and leave the details of personality and character to be supplied by the individual, depending on his personal tastes.

How often people say, "Oh, I don't think God would do that," or "I'm sure God isn't that way," about something clearly taught in Scripture! God said, "I AM WHO I AM" (Exod. 3:14). His character is absolute and unchanging. Our opinions are useless—worse than useless, in fact, if they keep us satisfied with false impressions and dull our desire to learn the truth. The longing of the Christian should be, like Paul, to know Christ (Phil. 3:10).

It is my hope and prayer that we will grow in our understanding of God the Father as we continue in this book. But we must realize that the task of learning what God is really like will never be completed in this life, but will extend from time into eternity. Nevertheless, the more time we spend meditating on Scripture that reveals the personality of the Father, the more natural a part of our lives His attributes will become. The Holy Spirit is waiting to reveal to us the mind of God (John 16:13; 1 Cor. 2:12) and to replace false ideas with the truth.

God, of course, has many attributes that humans can never claim. A mother can never be all-knowing (despite her children's suspicions when she seems to see through walls), everywhere present, or without beginning or end. No father is all-powerful, invisible, or completely just. We will never become as godly a parent as we would like, no matter how hard we study or try.

Nevertheless, God has given to us the responsibility of parenthood and has put us in authority over our children. Since we know He never requires of us more than that which, by His grace, He has already supplied, we can go forward confidently. Our Father God will reveal His true nature to us and help us become His kind of mother. "For he knows how we are formed, he remembers that we are dust" (Ps. 103:14). As He said to Paul, so He says to us, "My grace is sufficient for you, for my power is made perfect in weakness" (2 Cor. 12:9).

Making It Personal

1. When you think of God, what mental picture do you have?

_____

_____

_____

2. How has your earthly father influenced your ideas about your heavenly Father? _____

_____

_____

_____

3. What does the world think God is like? _____

_____

_____

_____

4. Why is it important for us to know what God is like?

_____

_____

_____

5. List as many characteristics of God as you can find in this chapter. _____

_____

_____

_____

6. What picture of God do you get from Psalm 103? _____

_____

Before you read on. . . . Do you feel your father and mother really loved you? Why do you feel this way? / If your mother was not a loving person, what could be the result? Read Ezekiel 16:44-45. / If we did not experience love in our home, how can we fill that void now? Read John 15:9 and Romans 5:5. / Did you want the number of children you have? / Is love more a matter of *feeling* or of *doing*? Read 1 Corinthians 13:4-7 with this in mind.

4

GOD'S KIND OF LOVE

In Titus 2:4, the main thing women are encouraged to do for their children is to love them. At another time in history this might seem to be a superfluous suggestion. Of course mothers love their children! They don't need to be told to do that! But in today's world we often see beneath the thin veneer of socially accepted behavior, and we come to realize that all mothers do not love their children, at least not in any recognizable way. This must have been true in Paul's day, too, or God would not have used him to urge mothers to do so. Many women in my classes have also shared their doubts about whether their mothers really loved them.

If a couple has had a difficult time conceiving or has had to wait several years for a child, chances are that any child born or adopted into their family will be much loved. But if a child is unplanned, often he or she is viewed as a hindrance to financial or career plans, as an inconvenience, or even as an embarrassment, for example, if the couple is unmarried. In other cases, children are simply accepted as a normal and inevitable occurrence in life, with no thought to their being special or precious in any way.

Before we can love our children with God's kind of love, we must see our children with God's eyes. In Psalm 127:3, God says, "Behold, children are a gift of the LORD; the fruit of the womb is a reward" (NASB). And despite the cries from those who feel parents should limit the number of children they have, God goes on to say in verses 4-5, "Like arrows in the hand of a warrior, so are the children of one's youth. How blessed is the man whose quiver is full of them; they shall not be ashamed, when they speak with their enemies in the gate" (NASB). Children are to be viewed, then, as a gift from the Lord—a reward, a blessing, and a source of strength as we face our enemies.

I cringe inwardly when I hear a mother refer to her child as "our little mistake" or other half-joking, but disparaging designations. How much better to have the attitude of Jacob when he introduced his children to his brother, Esau: "They are the children God has graciously given your servant" (Gen. 33:5). If we know that God knew Jeremiah before He formed him in the womb, and if we believe that "in all things God works for the good of those who love him, who have been called according to his purpose" (Rom. 8:28), then we are clearly out of God's will if we do not accept our children as loving gifts from a loving Father.

God's kind of love can come only from God Himself (1 John 4:7). We cannot manufacture it on our own. Love is part of the fruit of the Spirit (Gal. 5:22), and it is to Him we must go to receive godly love for our children. If we have wrong attitudes toward our children and we confess them to God, He will forgive us and fill us. "And hope does not disappoint us, because God has poured out his love into our hearts by the Holy Spirit, whom he has given us" (Rom. 5:5).

Undeserved Love

When we see our children with God's eyes, then we can begin to love our children with God's kind of love, a love that is *undeserved*. In Deuteronomy 7:6-10, God says there was nothing about the people of Israel that made them especially appealing. They could offer Him nothing. He specifically says He did not choose them because of their size or influence, for He says they were fewer than anyone else. In Romans, we are told that God demonstrated His love for us while we were still unlovable, unlikable sinners (5:8)—and most of us were not even Jewish sinners, at that. We are loved, not because we are a certain color, or because we are more intelligent, or more polite, or better looking. God just loves us.

In the same way, our children should never have to earn our love. When they are born or adopted into our family, we do not love them because they have some inborn quality or special attribute that makes them worthy of our love. We love them because they belong to us and because, like God at creation, we desire to have someone on whom to shower our love, someone to be on the receiving end of all the special emotions that well up within both the father and the mother in a normal situation. God the Father loves each of His children this way, and this is the response He gives us toward our children.

Self-giving Love

God's kind of love is also *self-giving*. "For God so loved the world that he gave . . ." (John 3:16); "I live by faith in the Son of God, who loved me and gave himself for me" (Gal. 2:20). It is this kind of self-giving love that Jesus had in mind when He said, "A new commandment I give to you: Love one another. As I have loved you, so you must love one another" (John 13:34).

Expressing self-giving love toward our children comes naturally to most parents. Jesus said that even those who are evil know how to give good gifts to their children (Matt. 7:11). Traditionally, parents have hoped to provide their children with more advantages than they had, and they have been willing to sacrifice in order to attain this goal.

In recent years, however, the mood has changed. Parents are often caught up in such a quest for self-fulfillment that children are expected to fit in with their parents' plans and cope the best they can. The idea of sacrificing for one's children is not popular. If the state will not step in and provide recreational and educational opportunities, if the church or community does not organize programs to take care of problem areas, if a child's needs conflict with a parent's needs, the child is the one who suffers.

Fortunately, God does not act on the basis of what is easiest for Him or what He can get out of it, but on the basis of meeting us in our need. If we would be godly mothers, we must follow His pattern and reach out to our children in self-giving love even at some cost to ourselves. We probably will never be required to give our lives for our children as

Jesus gave His for us, but we can demonstrate that we understand what this kind of love means by doing those things that will tell our children that they have supreme worth in our eyes.

Steadfast Love

God's kind of love is not only undeserved and self-giving, it is *steadfast.* Psalm 118 repeats the phrase "His steadfast love endures forever" (RSV) many times. *Steadfast* means "fixed, unchanging, constant." God's love lasts forever.

Our love for our children should not depend on our mood at a given moment. Our children should be able to trust us to always have their best interests at heart; they should be secure in their place in our lives. The pressures of life and our human frailties make it difficult for us as parents to express steadfast love as continuously as we know we should.

One of the houses we lived in had beautiful hydrangea bushes which would bloom each year, their foot-wide masses of blossoms constituting the most dramatic attraction of our landscaping. When one of our sons was about four years old, he came into the kitchen one day and held up his little pail so I could see the results of his morning's activity. Inside the pail lay the newly sprouted, still-closed buds of perhaps twenty hydrangea blossoms. He had picked the backyard bushes bare.

I blew a fuse. I ranted and raved. I spanked him. I sent him to his room. I was beside myself with anger and frustration. It took me over an hour to get anywhere near calmed down. At that point I began to tell myself that such a little boy had no idea of the scope of his act, that the little green knobs were no different to him than the pods on the mimosa or the berries on other bushes that he was allowed to pick. I started to feel that I should go and apologize for my overwrought state.

I went to my son's room, sat on his bed, and put him on my

lap. I explained about what lovely bushes we would have had if he had not picked the buds. "But," I said, "I should not have gotten so mad at you and I'm sorry I did." My son then proceeded to finish me off by saying in a kindly voice, "That's all right, mommy. Jesus still loves me."

Yes, God's love is steadfast and unchanging, and a mother's love should be, also.

Learning Divine Love

Divine love, of course, goes beyond any human affection, beyond even the deep bond between parent and child. In 1 Corinthians 13, we find the most clear biblical explanation of this higher love, love which cannot coexist with the self-centeredness that is common to all of us, including mothers. Divine love

is patient	is not irritable or resentful
is kind	does not rejoice at wrong
is not jealous	rejoices in the right
does not boast	bears all things
is not arrogant	believes all things
is not rude	hopes all things
	endures all things

This list is not meant to discourage us but to reveal to us that God's kind of love is not shallow sentimentality. Love means *doing* more than *feeling,* for God knows that *as we do loving acts, loving relationships will result and loving feelings will grow.* Our love for our children will increase as we involve ourselves with them in a patient, kindly, hopeful, cheerful, self-giving manner, and as we pray for the Holy Spirit to pour God's love into our hearts.

To learn to love is as important for the mother as for the child, for according to this passage of Scripture, none of us is anything if we do not have love (v. 2). We may be intelligent, industrious, clever, well-meaning, and even biblically knowledgeable, but if love is missing, we cannot be to our families what God intends for us to be. If we have a lack in this area, we must pray with David of old, "Create in me a clean heart, O God, and put a new and right spirit within me" (Ps. 51:10 RSV). God will meet us in our need and cause our love for our children to grow until it reflects ever more clearly the perfect love of God Himself.

Making It Personal

1. What sometimes hinders parents' love for children? (Be sure to include Ezekiel 16:44-45 here along with other ideas.)

_____

_____

_____

2. What should be our attitude toward our children? _____

_____

_____

_____

3. Where can we get a proper love for our children? _____

_____

_____

_____

4. Discuss the three aspects of God's kind of love outlined in the chapter. _____

_____

_____

_____

5. Look up 1 Corinthians 13 in several translations and list the attributes of love. How can we keep from being discouraged at our failures in love? _____

_____

_____

_____

_____

6. How important is it to learn to love (1 Cor. 13:2)? _____

_____

_____

_____

7. Do you feel loving emotion toward your children? If not, ask God to help you love your children. Read 1 John 4:7.

_____

_____

_____

8. Does true love for children include setting limits? How can we be sure of this? See Genesis 2:16–17; Exodus 20:7–17. _

_____

_____

9. How do you reconcile Psalm 103:14 with Hebrews 12:6?

_____

_____

Before you read on. . . . Was the family of your childhood affectionate? / Which do your children hear most from you: words of love and cheer, or words of anger and disapproval? / Do your children know you love them? / How much time do you spend in companionship with each of your children? / Is your discipline done in love?

5

HOW IS GOD'S KIND OF LOVE EXPRESSED?

There is an old story about a girl who came home from school in rapture, exclaiming, "Oh, mother! Now I know Billy Duncan loves me!"

"How do you know?"

"He pushed me down the stairs!"

This kind of attention may satisfy some adolescent hearts, but shoving can hardly be thought of as the universal language of love. However, this adolescent did grasp one truth—love is communicated *physically*.

Physical Expressions of Love

In chapter 2 we saw that God pictured Himself carrying His little child on His hip and fondling it on His knees (Isa. 66:12-13). What a tender, personal description of healthy parental love this is! In the New Testament we find that Jesus laid His hands on children while He blessed them; and the waiting father, who represents God in the parable, embraced the returning prodigal son and kissed him.

As these and other passages illustrate, family members are not supposed to be untouchable to each other. There should be freedom to extend the comforting hand, give one another affectionate hugs, and exchange kisses. Our world is full of affection-starved individuals, people hungry for caring human contact. Too often mothers and fathers feel they have fulfilled their parental duties by meeting the material needs of their children while neglecting their children's emotional requirements, which are just as real.

When our first son was born, there was such an overload at the hospital that after delivery they rolled me in as the seventh bed in a six-bed ward. When feeding time came, I was so excited looking down at my newborn baby that without even thinking of what I was doing, I started pouring out all kinds of motherly gibberish: "Aren't you sweet? I love you so much. You're exactly what I wanted. Do you miss me in the nursery? I could hardly wait to hold you," and so on. During the whole time, I was looking at his tiny hands and fingernails, his feet and toenails, and brushing the wisps of hair around on his head. All of a sudden, I stopped. Looking around, I realized I was the only person in the room making any noise at all. The other women were sitting absolutely still in bed, just holding their bundles. I felt foolish, wondering what all the other mothers thought about my rapturous monologue.

Since then I have often pondered that scene. I hope the other women were just too overwhelmed to move, at only a temporary loss for words. For it seems to me that an ability to express intimate, satisfying maternal love begins here. We must cuddle our children and coo at them from the start, or later we may feel so awkward that we avoid initiating the kind of physical contact that will meet both their needs and ours.

Verbal Expressions of Love

God's kind of love is also expressed *verbally*. Jesus continually told His disciples that He loved them (John 15). God spoke of His love for the Israelites over and over again. We need to be reminded that we are loved by God because we are aware of our wandering ways and know He has a right to be angry with us.

In the same way, our children must be reassured constantly and verbally that we love them. They need to know that their mistakes and disobedience, as well as the ensuing discipline, have not alienated us from them. They need to be reminded that our love for them is not dependent on their flawlessly maintaining some standard of behavior, and that we will continue to love them no matter what.

Such love often will seem too much for them to hope for, just as God's love for us is beyond all understanding. That is why we all need to be reminded verbally that it nevertheless exists. The confidence this knowledge creates in children does not make them more careless about their conduct. Instead, their security in their parents' love frees them from basic anxieties so they can concentrate on pleasing those in authority over them and enjoying a far more carefree childhood.

I have found that showing physical and verbal love to teen-age boys is much the same as catching giraffes: you wait until they come to feed, and get them while they are off-balance. Giving one of my six-foot sons a hug and saying, "I love you, babe," satisfies some deep need in me, as well as in him. Being able to express love makes life worth living. If we do not overcome whatever hesitation toward verbal and physical expressions of love we may have carried over from our own upbringing, our children will be emotionally handicapped, and will more than likely carry the same inability into their own adulthood.

Time and Attention

God also expresses His love for us by *the things He does for us.* In creation He prepared a world perfectly suited to our needs. Every requirement for our physical well-being was graciously provided. When man sinned, this perfect setting was marred, and from that time mankind has had to sweat and struggle to gain even a measure of the comfort that would have been ours automatically otherwise. Even so, the beauty of the earth and sky and the very elements of our atmosphere still meet our physical and emotional needs.

We, too, prove our love for our children by the kinds of things we do for them. Providing them with as comfortable an environment as our means will allow without acting as if we begrudge the money and efforts it costs us is just the beginning of our task. Remembering special days, occasionally cooking their favorite meals, buying the outfits that they like best, even if they aren't always such a super bargain—all these kinds of actions tell our children they are more than just a necessary evil we put up with. When one of my children finds me baking something special and asks, "Are you going to a potluck tonight?" it is a pretty good indication that they have been getting short-changed as far as my interest and time are concerned.

Fortunately, God did not just create us and then lose interest. He has always shown His love for His people by *being with them* wherever He led them. The Israelites could see the cloud by day and the pillar of fire by night to reassure them that God was in their midst. Jesus, whose name *Immanual* means "God with us," spent thirty-three years with us to prove God loves us, and lived day and night with the disciples for three of those years. In addition to that, He is available to us every moment and has promised never to leave us or forsake us.

Likewise, our children know we care deeply for them when we are willing to spend time with them. If we are constantly pushing them off onto babysitters, if we don't make the effort to go to their programs at school and church, if we can't find the time to read them a story or talk with them or pray with them, they have a right to wonder if we really love them. Just as it is difficult to imagine a couple in love who never want to spend time together, so our verbal protestations will ring hollow if we do not make opportunities to spend time with the children we claim to love.

Sacrificial Love

God not only provides for us and spends time with us, He "demonstrates his own love toward us in this: While we were still sinners, Christ died for us" (Rom. 5:8). No greater proof of God's love can be imagined; and the sacrifices we are willing to make for our children will be some indication of the depth of our devotion for them, also. These sacrifices are not always evident to the youngster, at least not until he or she reaches adulthood and understands the real cost of many things which were simply taken for granted; certainly Christians can only begin to perceive the price Jesus paid on the cross. But we as parents know if we are really willing to deny ourselves for our children, and whether we want to admit it or not, our children can also sense our deficiencies in this area, particularly as they grow older.

Discipline

Finally, God expresses His love to His children through *discipline*. In Hebrews 12:6 we are told, ". . . the Lord disciplines those he loves, and he punishes everyone he accepts as a son."

Unfortunately, some mothers feel that they are showing love for their children if they protect them from spankings and other disciplinary action. Exactly the opposite is true. Proverbs 13:24 goes so far as to say, "He who spares the rod hates his son, but he who loves him is careful to discipline him."

Far from urging parents to be lenient, the Bible clearly commands, "Do not withhold discipline from a child . . ." (Prov. 23:13). A reason for this is given, also. "The rod and reproof give wisdom, but a child who gets his own way brings shame to his mother" (29:15).

Therefore, we see that discipline is for the good of both the child and the parents. Neither will enjoy the kind of life God wants for those who belong to Him if the child is allowed to be disobedient. God demands that believers obey Him, and we must follow His lead and require obedience from our children, also.

Psychologists tell us that the opposite of love is not hate or anger but indifference. Just as God's discipline to us proves He accepts us as sons, our discipline shows our children how much we care about them.

"But," you may argue, "You just got through pointing out how real love is patient and kind, how it bears and endures all things. Maybe my child's misbehavior is one of the things

God wants me to endure. If I spank my child, I'm not bearing all things, am I?"

That is not the question. The question is: Whose character is God interested in? Yours alone? Or is God also concerned about the character of that little dynamo running around your house? Certainly you are supposed to be patient and kind, but so is each of your children.

How will Junior learn to be courteous if he is allowed to be rude? How will he grow up to be humble if he is habitually arrogant as a child? When will he learn to bear all things himself if he has never had to bear anything at all?

If we do not discipline our children, either out of laziness, lack of courage, or some false sense of increasing our own spirituality, we are denying them the opportunity to develop the kind of character that God admires. We are also preventing them from becoming the kind of individuals other people enjoy. How sad if our child should incur the displeasure of both God and man because of our refusal to discipline him!

One of the mothers in a class for mothers I have been teaching echoed the experience of many who have insisted on obedience in a consistent way for the first time: "We had a terrible week. No matter what I said, he did the opposite. I spanked him so many times I literally felt sick. Finally, on the fifth day, after about the third spanking, there was a lull. I was reading a magazine, trying to recuperate, when my son came to me, put his arms around my neck, and said, 'I love you, mommy.'"

Our children themselves want us to be courageous enough to subdue them. A weak parent is frightening to a child. "If she can't even handle me," they have a right to reason, "how can she protect me when something really big comes up?"

Our heavenly Father has set the patterns for exhibiting love physically, verbally, through actions, and through discipline. If we ourselves are obedient children, we will endeavor to do what is pleasing to Him in our role as mothers. If we will determine to overcome any past impediments and follow God's example, He will help us meet our children's inner needs and bless our every effort to express His kind of love.

Making It Personal

1. Identify five ways love is expressed. How does God express love to us in these same ways? _____

_____

_____

_____

_____

_____

2. What would happen if we omitted any one of these ways (i.e., expressed love verbally but not physically, and so on)?

_____

_____

_____

3. How did your parents express love to you? _____

_____

_____

4. In what ways do you express love to your children?

_____

_____

_____

_____

5. What does discipline express? Why do some mothers hesitate to discipline? _____

_____

_____

_____

6. Is your discipline done in love? _____

_____

_____

_____

7. How can a cold, unemotional mother become the loving person God desires? (Eph. 4:22–24; Rom. 5:5.) _____

_____

_____

_____

8. How should a mother deal with inner bitterness that causes her to say and do unkind things to her children? (Eph. 4:29–32.) _____

_____

_____

_____

9. What can we learn about love and its expression from 1 John 4:7–21? _____

_____

_____

Before you read on. . . . Where did you learn about the forms of discipline you use? / What forms of discipline do you use most often? / Do you ever put things off because you don't feel like doing them? / Are your habits under control? / Are *you* a disciplined person, a good example for your children? / Do you think teen-age rebellion is unavoidable?

6

PREVENTIVE DISCIPLINE

When one noted speaker was asked how children should be disciplined, he replied, "The only two things I find mentioned in the Bible are the rod and reproof." While these certainly are found in Scripture, we also find many other methods of discipline that are biblically sound, since they are utilized by God the Father and demonstrated in the life of Christ. Discipline should not be viewed only as punishment, but *as every means employed by parents to promote correct behavior and develop right attitudes in their children.* We will refer to these two aspects as *preventive* discipline and *corrective* discipline.

When a baby first begins to crawl, stand, and explore, he is too young to understand carefully reasoned explanations about why he should not climb on certain objects or touch certain articles. A mother may pick up the child and carry him to the far end of the house, but without discipline before long Junior will find his way, like a homing pigeon, right back to the forbidden item and attempt to continue what he was doing before he was interrupted. At this age, smacking a child's hands or bottom and issuing one- or two-word commands are about the only effective means of getting the mother's point across. She must realize the crucial importance of winning these first contests of the will, or Junior will wear her down with his single-minded determination; and every disciplinary encounter from that point on will be more difficult because of her earlier laxity.

But as a child develops, there are many other ways a parent can encourage correct conduct, methods that will sometimes, at least, make the rod and reproof unnecessary. The first two forms of preventive discipline are closely linked and must be used together to be effective. They are *teaching* and *example.*

Teaching and example are without a doubt the most difficult disciplinary "techniques" to master. They are hard because we have to know something before we can teach it, and we have to shape up our own lives before we can set the proper example. Saying "Do as I say, not as I do" never produced righteous living in anyone.

Teaching

The entire Old Testament is the story of God's trying to teach His people His ways, their obedience or disobedience, and God's expressions of pleasure or displeasure. In Deuteronomy 6:7, Proverbs 3:1, and Jeremiah 11:7-8, as well as elsewhere in Scripture, the important role of instructing and receiving instruction is outlined. The teaching of correct behavior by the parent before reproof is needed is a constant obligation. It is to be continued diligently "when you sit at home and when you walk along the road, when you lie down and when you get up" (Deut. 6:7). No wonder discipline seems to take so much of a parent's time! But God's command is plain. Parents are expected not only to *know* what behavior is pleasing to the Lord, but are to communicate continuously that knowledge to their offspring so that other forms of discipline will not be needed as often.

The demand of such teaching on a mother's time is enormous. If she has several children, she must repeat the same instruction over again as each reaches higher levels of understanding, or else younger children will miss many valuable and necessary lessons. Perhaps the reason many younger children exhibit undesirable behavior is that their mothers have neglected to repeat vital information and are less careful than they were with older children to insist on strict obedience.

An incident in our family illustrates this perfectly. When our two older boys, who are one year apart in age, became interested in skateboards, their father vetoed the idea. We knew of several children who had suffered severe injuries on skateboards, and my husband did not think the benefit received from having them was worth the risk. The decision was plain: they were not to ride skateboards. The matter was settled.

Three or four years later, we got a call from the sponsor of our junior youth group. Our third son had been experimenting on a skateboard that one of the other youngsters had used to get to club, had fallen off, and seemed to be in a great deal of pain. We took him to our doctor and found out he had a broken collarbone. When we asked him why he had gotten on the skateboard when they were forbidden, he replied that he thought we were against skateboards because they cost too much; he didn't realize he wasn't allowed to ride those belonging to others. His punishment could not have been worse. Trussed up in a halter for eight weeks, he couldn't help his team in their Little League play-off the next Saturday, and sat on the sidelines while his team lost the championship.

Then, not more than a few weeks later, our four-year-old daughter came in crying and holding her mouth. She had taken a spill trying to ride a skateboard belonging to a boy down the street. Her front tooth turned dark but was, fortunately, a baby tooth and we only had to look at it day in and day out for two years.

Teaching and re-teaching is a time-consuming task, but knowing what to teach is also difficult. Schools and community groups hold seminars for parents, but these will not provide all the answers, for each of their suggested tactics and standards of behavior must be held up to the Word of God to see if it contains truth or merely reflects some current cultural fad.

Example

But even conscientious instruction is not enough. Mothers cannot be teachers or hearers of truth only, but must be "doers of the word" or else they "deceive themselves" (James 1:22). That is why the second disciplinary tool is essential if our teaching is not to be in vain. It is easy to overlook our own failings and bad habits while nagging our children about theirs. Parents may be late to their own appointments without a second thought, but they have a fit when their children are late to dinner or school. Adults may leave projects or clothes strewn around the house while insisting that their children put away one toy before getting out the next. Some mothers and fathers have what can only be called temper tantrums but don't allow their children to show anger.

God knew that more than teaching would be required, so when all of His instruction in the Old Testament failed to get across His true nature and desires, Jesus Christ came, not only to continue the teaching and to be the sacrifice for our sins, but also to demonstrate the kind of living that pleases God.

We are understandably shaken when commanded to "be perfect, as your heavenly Father is perfect" (Matt. 5:48), for to demonstrate that level of living seems to be possible only to the Son of God Himself. But Paul urged believers several times to "follow my example, as I follow the example of Christ" (1 Cor. 11:1; see also, 4:16; Phil. 3:17). Because the same Power available to Paul is available to us, we cannot shrug off as impossible our responsibility to live godly lives.

It is the combination of word and deed, then—precept and example—that composes the most potent form of preventive discipline available to the parent. One without the other is inadequate. If we were to live a good life without explaining why we act as we do, we would leave our children with dangerously uninformed opinions, with conclusions arrived at by guesswork. On the other hand, teaching correct doctrine without maintaining disciplined behavior ourselves consti-tutes hypocrisy and may cause those watching us to become cynical and unbelieving.

I have observed with interest that some of the harshest public schoolteachers and principals, the ones who punished the most severely for minor offenses, were those whose own lack of personal morality was common knowledge among their colleagues. I often wondered what I would say to my children if they found out what they were really like. I am sure they would have felt more resentful of discipline received from them and more suspicious of others in authority.

We have heard for many years about the drop-out rate within the evangelical church among children of church members. The fact that so many young people from Christian families display so little commitment caused me to have recurring fears about our ability to guide our children safely into Christian adulthood. As the years have passed, I have come to believe that it must be the dichotomy between what children are taught at church and what they experience at home that sours them. There must be a large number of active, Bible-believing Christian fathers and mothers who are hypocrites without even knowing it, nodding in hearty agreement with biblical principles at church, but living worldly lives at home.

Even some evangelical churches have been content to preach salvation and support missionaries while the families within them die for lack of specific, powerful instruction on how to live together as Christians. A few even seem to brag about being the "fightin'est, lovin'est bunch of people around," which is hardly the sort of church the New Testament recommends.

For most people, it is much more comfortable to study about prayer, witnessing, or the end times than it is to have to learn how to be a godly mother, father, husband, or wife. Thankfully, many programs and books have emerged during the last few years to help couples meet this most crucial need. The truth is, if our church families do not increasingly reflect the nature of God, they, as well as the world, must become our mission field.

It has been fashionable to say that all children must rebel against their parents in order to mature into complete adults, and Christians have often accepted this worldly conclusion as truth. But in light of God's Word and His condemnation of the rebellious child, we should reconsider this view. Of course each healthy child must grow into independence, but surely God does not decree that in order to grow up young people must incur God's wrath by rebelling against their parents!

It is too easy for parents to say, "Oh, well, they have to rebel sooner or later. That's just the way it is." This covers up a lot of poor parenting. With this attitude, a child who falls away from the church and rejects Christ is often referred to as doing what is "normal" and expected. This is even more dangerous a view when we realize that *most of us tend to do what we think others expect us to do.* The parent is simultaneously sending signals to his child that he expects the child to rebel, while providing himself with a ready-made excuse when it happens.

It is God's plan that children instead be nurtured by instruction and example in such a way that they can make the transition from dependence to independence without the sin of rebellion. Parents who not only teach the necessary precepts, but show in their daily living the joy, peace, and clear conscience that come with obeying those precepts, will be making any other sort of life seem too fraught with instability and unhappiness to be appealing. This is especially true when the disciplinary tools of teaching and example are joined with a third: *praise.*

Praise

Despite our notions to the contrary, expressing praise does not come naturally to most people, especially parents. More often we act as if we believe that if children do all that is required of them and give us no trouble, they are only doing as they ought and deserve no special recognition. It is only when they get out of line or perturb us that they come to our attention. Yet if we stop to think about our own reactions, most of us bend over backwards trying to please someone who praises our efforts. On the other hand, we feel defeated in the presence of those who are critical of us.

The women in the classes I teach often find it difficult to complete one of the projects assigned for the fifth week, that of praising each of their children (and their husbands) for at least one positive action each day. It is not that there are no good deeds to commend, but the days just slip away in their normal pattern, which usually includes no praise for anyone.

How tragic this is, when praise is perhaps the easiest, most joyful, and most productive method of preventive discipline in existence. All you have to do is catch someone doing something right one time, compliment him on it, and you practically insure its becoming a permanent part of his behavior—after the shock wears off, at least. This technique is a part of what psychologists term "reinforcing desirable behavior."

As Christians we often look forward to the day when, wonder of wonders, Christ may say to us, "Well done, good and faithful servant!" (Matt. 25:21). The assurance that we have the approval of our Lord keeps us plugging when the going gets rough. In the same way, children, even more susceptible to suggestion, are spurred on to great heights of effort by a simple "What a good job you are doing cleaning your room" or "Your handwriting on this paper is great!"

Your words, however, must be carefully chosen and *never* carry the underlying negative message of "Finally!" or "Why don't you do this all the time?" The implied criticism of poorly worded comments will turn intended praise into more condemnation and mar the enjoyment of the task well done.

To think that we may "spoil" children or make them difficult to work with by praising them is a dreadful misconception. Does praise spoil you? Do you become insufferable when people tell you they like your work? When a child says, "That sure was a good dinner, mom," do you respond by serving slop the next night, or by trying even harder? Most of us are involved in daily situations that make us feel inferior or inadequate, and children are no exception. The few compliments we receive along the way are cups of cool water in a desert.

Praise is a Christian activity. Praise, as long as it is honest, feeds our spirits and our children's, and engenders a healthy self-image that promotes success instead of failure. Mothers should vow to compliment their children whenever they have an opportunity to do so. Their relationships with their children will improve, their youngsters will begin feeling good about themselves, and the need for other, less attractive means of discipline will be reduced.

When our daughter was small, she had a habit of picking at her fingernails, especially when ill at ease. When I saw her doing it, I would reach out and take one of her hands in mine or say quietly, "Don't pick your nails, dear." I also spoke to her about it in private, but she did not seem able to stop. One day after teaching the class session on praising children, I decided my tactics had been all wrong. So I kept an eye on her hands, and one day I spied a fingernail with a quarter of an inch of white on the tip. "What a beautiful fingernail you have!" I exclaimed, careful not to infer any criticism of the other nails. For the next few weeks, she would come show me her fingernails as they were growing and I would enjoy them with her. Within five weeks all ten nails were so long I had to start filing them down.

All situations, of course, do not resolve themselves so neatly. But there can be no doubt that much more behavior can be changed through praise than most of us realize. When you add to that the amount of good conduct that can be strengthened and made permanent simply by being commended, it is ridiculous that Christian parents think to use the method so seldom.

Little effort is expended by saying, "That's a good idea. You often have helpful ideas"; or, "I appreciate the way you asked to be excused before leaving the table. It shows you have good manners." If nothing else, such comments make our children aware that *we actually do see the good things they do and appreciate them,* which will make them more accepting of our correction when they have done something wrong.

Control the Environment

A fourth way to keep our children from getting into trouble is to *control their environment* until they have the ability to cope successfully with problems of increasing difficulty on their own.

A small child cannot be trusted to stay safely on the curb and never step in front of an oncoming car. He does not understand death, nor does he know the limitations of cars and drivers. In order to keep him safe, a fenced play area should be provided; and it will take an alert mother to keep him inside of that. On a less serious level, because all art projects of preschoolers in our home have been conducted in the kitchen, we have never yet had a wall redecorated by any of our children. Our toddlers had their drawer in the kitchen that they could get into any time they wished. Since it was filled with safe but delightfully noisy utensils and pans, they were content with the demand that they leave all other cupboards alone. Many exasperating moments can be prevented with a little parental forethought.

So much emphasis has been placed on the importance of the mother's being at home with her children until they start school that many seem to underestimate the need of young people of all ages to have proper supervision. Many parents seem to have no qualms about allowing their adolescent children to fend for themselves every day after school. But the kinds of trouble adolescents might become involved in can have at least as disastrous consequences as those of three-year-olds. Our teen-agers need to have their environments controlled, also. They may be whizzes in math or other subjects at school, but despite the open discussion of sex, drugs, and other tantalizing topics, *they are no more able to cope with these maturely on their own than young people ever have been.*

When we pray, "Lead us not into temptation," we are asking God to control our environment, even as supposedly mature adults. In 1 Corinthians 10:13 we are promised that our loving Father will see to it that we are never tempted beyond our strength.

As parents, we must protect our children from situations they are not capable of handling alone. Whether this means removing an expensive dish from the table where a toddler might grab it, arranging to be home when our children are not in school, or setting firm dating limits, it is up to the parent to foresee potentially dangerous circumstances and take the precautions necessary to insure that their child is not led into temptation but is preserved from evil.

Warning

A fifth tactic for promoting desired behavior found in Scripture is *warning*. Throughout the Old Testament, God graciously warned His people of the dangers of disobedience, and Jesus continued the pattern in His teaching.

Several popular child psychologists tell us we should never say, "If you do that again, you will get a spanking," because, they claim , one should never threaten a child. But this is to confuse threat and intimidation with warning. To threaten implies the use of extreme fear of severe pain or injury. A threat is intended to benefit the one who gives the threat at the expense of the one who receives it.

In contrast, a warning is a healthy reminder that breaking a moral, spiritual, or natural law will bring about some certain and predictable negative result that we would like to spare the one we are warning. It was kind of God to warn Adam and Eve that they would die if they disobeyed Him; He did not take some malicious delight in proclaiming the inevitability of their death if they broke His command. It was a loving Father's heart that set before the children of Israel the blessings of obedience contrasted with the curses of disobedience as they were about to enter the Promised Land (Deut. 28). In the same way, a loving mother warns her child in the hope that disobedience and punishment may be avoided.

When we were touring Israel, we visited the archaeological tell of Meggido. As we approached the crest of the tell to look out over the Plain of Meggido (its lush farmland seems far removed from the Battle of Armaggedon that will one day rage there) we encountered Hebrew signs we could not read, but huge red exclamation marks made their meaning clear. We were not to go beyond those signs or some danger—in this case, the giving away of the earth near the edge—might befall us. We did not feel threatened; we felt protected. We were grateful for the warning.

A mother expresses love and concern for her children by warning them about the unpleasant consequences of wrong behavior. To do less would be irresponsible. Whether the results of their actions would mean the loss of a friend, physical injury, or punishment by the parent, a child has a right to the greater wisdom and foresight his mother and father possess. Cutting a child adrift in our complicated world to learn by trial and error alone would be heartless and cruel. He, too, will feel protected by carefully placed warnings and will be kept from unnecessary harm.

Rewards

A sixth biblical encouragement for right living is the giving of *rewards*. This practice, another means of "reinforcing desirable behavior," is also in ill repute among many experts, possibly because it can be, and often is, misused. But Jesus shamelessly declared that some actions will bring great reward in heaven, and His parables often illustrated rewards of all kinds.

For mothers, the biggest problem is taking care that they are actually rewarding the behavior they think they are rewarding. For example, if you offer a child a piece of candy to make her stop crying, you are actually rewarding her for crying. If she wants another piece of candy, she reasons, she should start crying, and someone will give her one to get her to stop.

The greatest reward a parent can give—and the one that is craved the most by children—*is attention.* Therefore, the parent must be careful what kind of conduct on the part of their children succeeds in capturing their attention most often. The child who doesn't receive parental praise and recognition for positive actions will undoubtedly resort to disobedience, crying, clowning, constant talking, or some other ploy in order to satisfy his need for his parent to notice him.

In Matthew 6:1-6, Jesus promises that God will reward those who act in a proper way in spiritual matters. In the Beatitudes, He outlines specific rewards for specific attitudes (Matt. 5:3-10). In Matthew 16:15-17, He pronounces a blessing on Peter for merely verbalizing a truth revealed to him from heaven. Therefore, as parents, we see that material goods are not the only, nor even the primary, payment for pleasing God. The knowledge that we have pleased Him as well as unseen, sometimes future, spiritual blessings are most commonly promised.

Nevertheless, in Matthew 25:20-21, in Jesus' parable about the servants and the talents, we see that the reward was not only the master's pleasure, but also the tangible increase of responsibility: "You have been faithful with a few things; I will put you in charge of many things" (v. 21). From this we can conclude that *rewarding our children with new privileges and increased status* when they have been faithful in lesser tasks is a proper response.

Most of us do this more or less automatically, and this loses some of the power inherent in the situation. If we made more of an occasion over allowing a child later bedtime or the granting of some new privilege, we would increase the effectiveness of such steps with regard to future conduct. Our children should have reason to feel that they will be treated more maturely as they display more mature behavior and be given more privileges as they shoulder more responsibility. Their allowances should not be increased as a bribe or in order to appease, but as a recognition of greater need and a growing ability to handle money in a proper manner.

I personally do not think it wise to give children money for good grades on a report card. It is far better, I believe, for a child to learn the value of inner pride at a job well done and to bask in the obvious pleasure of his family, or else to link the child's successfully coping with the strains and requirements of his studies to some new privilege that rewards such mature behavior. Surveys show that adults rank the inner satisfaction of their jobs as more important than higher salaries. It has been my experience that children feel the same. Money is soon spent, but the emotional impact of knowing you have earned your own and others' commendation lingers on.

Small monetary rewards can sometimes be useful, especially with young children who have a greater need for immediate results from their actions. But even for them, a check or star on a chart often pleases them just as much.

Certainly children should be paid for performing extra, time-consuming chores around the house, those above and beyond their share of work required by daily family routine. The ability to earn additional money encourages initiative and increases a child's sense of power over the direction of his life.

But it should be remembered that the most important rewards an adult can give a child are praise, approval, and attention. If these are missing, all the money, treats, and trinkets in the world will not make up for the lack the child feels.

A mother has many methods of preventive discipline, then, at her disposal. She can encourage good behavior by teaching and example, through praise and controlling their environment, with warnings and rewards. Despite all these, her children will misbehave at times and need corrective discipline. But to use every means possible to prevent wrong actions is to be more like God the Father as He reveals Himself in Scripture; and knowing that we are acting in a godly manner brings to mothers a special joy of its own.

Making It Personal

1. How would you define discipline? _____

_____

_____

_____

2. Can you reason with a toddler? How do you get him to obey you? _____

_____

_____

_____

3. Why has the author called some techniques "preventive discipline"? _____

_____

_____

_____

4. List each of the six methods covered in the chapter, including the biblical basis for each technique. _____

_____

_____

_____

_____

_____

5. Which of the above methods are the most neglected in your dealings with your children? _____

_____

_____

6. Do you habitually express pleasure when your children do something right? _____

_____

_____

7. Will a mother always use the same disciplinary technique with each of her children (Prov. 17:10)? _____

_____

_____

8. How do we know it is right to discipline our children (Heb. 12:6–8)? _____

_____

_____

Before you read on. . . . What does the word *feminine* mean to you—ruffles and bows? flighty? seductive? / Read Proverbs 31:10-31. What adjectives describe this woman? / What adjectives would you use to describe yourself? / Do people (e.g., teachers, friends) often compliment you on the behavior of your children? / Do you feel you have control over your children? / Do your children obey one parent better than they do the other? If so, why?

7

WHERE THE RUBBER MEETS THE ROAD

Just the other day I was picking up some clothes at the dry cleaners and noticed a large, hand-printed sign thumbtacked beside a lower section of counter where clean laundry is often stacked. The sign said Please Do Not Stand On This Step. A well-dressed woman and her daughter entered, and the little girl immediately climbed up on the forbidden area. "Get down," her mother said. "That's what they have the sign for." The girl continued to stand there, occasionally eyeing her mother to see if her face showed signs of any further action. The mother did not say another word to the child, and she was still playing on the step when I left.

So we see that it is not enough to teach our children what is right, to model proper behavior ourselves (the mother obeyed the sign perfectly), to praise, warn, or reward. Our job as a parent is not complete until *the child has obeyed.* On the face of it, this seems obvious. But the truth is that all mothers occasionally, and some mothers habitually, fail at just this point.

Three Reasons for Failure

One reason for this may be that *we give our children too many orders about things that don't really matter* to us. Because of our feelings of inadequacy and a desire to look like the perfect mother, we may constantly be telling our children what to do, overcoercing them in trivial matters.

If this is the problem, we must understand that we are wrong to tell our children to do something or to stop doing something if it isn't important. We must save our commands for times when we really want them to obey, whether that is often or seldom, and then see to it that they do. To repeat, we should *never* give a child an order unless it matters enough to us that we will follow through and assure his obedience. Giving unheeded directions does not make you look like a *good* mother; it reveals you as a *weak* mother.

Another reason mothers leave the disciplinary job undone is they are often distracted between the time they tell the child to do something and the completion of the task. Their minds stray, the telephone rings, another child claims their attention.

This happens at times to all of us, but for some women it occurs so often as to be practically a way of life. Their minds are totally disorganized, and like children themselves, they have such a short attention span that they cannot carry any project through to completion without getting side-tracked.

To some, such fluttery personalities may seem to be the epitome of femininity. The women in my classes tell me that for them the word *feminine* holds such meanings as soft, smelling nice, quiet, gracious, curls, ruffles, noncompetitive, gentle, lovable, pretty, patient. The mental picture conjured up is rather that of a southern belle twirling her dainty parasol while surrounded by admiring beaus. This image may be charming, but it does not survive the realities of changing a dirty diaper or disciplining an active four-year-old.

By contrast, the same women found the wife and mother described in Proverbs 31:10-31 to be creative, industrious, dignified, organized, generous, calm, practical, fearless, smart, wise, kind, well-dressed, virtuous, hospitable, and thrifty. They were comforted to have Scripture affirm that the woman who "works with eager hands . . . provides food for her family . . . watches over the affairs of her household . . . is clothed with strength and dignity . . . speaks with wisdom" will be praised by her husband and children.

The delineations in this passage of Scripture make it clear that the kind of woman God admires is neither flighty nor haphazard. On the contrary, God approves of the woman who is in control, who accomplishes all the necessary tasks for her family in an orderly fashion, and who claims the respect of both her husband and children.

Women who have trouble following through with tasks or with the discipline of their children must ask the Lord to help them become more faithful and consistent. They must make the effort to *discipline their own impulses and actions* while they also check those of their children.

A third reason women ignore the fact that their children have not minded them is that *they hope to avoid confrontation*. They may be afraid their children won't like them if they demand obedience, or they may simply be the kind of person who always tries to find the easy, painless way out of any potentially unpleasant situation.

These women are hoping for the impossible. *Children do not grow to love those who are afraid to confront them; they come to despise them.* And there is no painless, pleasant way out of the kinds of confrontation children create when they decide to test the limits set down by their parents.

The most that timid mothers will gain is a postponement of the showdown to determine who will run the family—parents or children—and such a delay usually means that the problems involved are far more serious and disagreeable than the earlier ones they chose to ignore. It is far easier, in the long run, to tackle a recalcitrant six-year-old than a stubborn sixteen-year-old.

God's Principles

God has some solemn words for those who think they can neglect their God-appointed tasks with impunity: "Do not be deceived: God cannot be mocked. A man reaps what he sows" (Gal. 6:7).

What harvest can parents who are not firm in their discipline expect to reap?

"A foolish son brings grief to his father and bitterness to the one who bore him" (Prov. 17:25).

"A foolish son is his father's ruin" (Prov. 19:13).

"The rod and reproof give wisdom, but a child who gets his own way brings shame to his mother" (Prov. 29:15).

Parents who let their children have their own way can expect to reap *bitterness, grief, ruin,* and *shame.* This is a high price to pay for neglecting our responsibilities as mothers.

God demands maturity from women who bear children. He expects courage. Those of us who hope to take the easy way out, to avoid confrontation, or to cling to the freedom from responsibility of our unmarried years will have no one but ourselves to blame for the grief God says will surely come if we ignore His warnings.

But what if we determine to gain control over our children, impose proper discipline, and be obedient to God's commands regarding our children? What does God promise us then? To those who rear their children according to God's principles, He promises *peace, delight, respect,* and *hope* for the future.

"Discipline your son, and he will give you peace; he will bring delight to your soul" (Prov. 29:17).

"Moreover, we have all had human fathers who disciplined us and we respected them for it . . ." (Heb. 12:9).

"Train a child in the way he should go, and even when he is old he will not turn from it" (Prov. 22:6).

Children have just as much to gain from being properly disciplined as parents do—perhaps more, if their lives run the normal course, since they will have more years to enjoy the fruits of their obedience than their elders. For Scripture promises much to young people who respond positively to authority.

"Honor your father and your mother, so that you may live long in the land the LORD your God is giving you" (Exod. 20:12).

"No discipline seems pleasant at the time, but painful. Later on, however, it produces a harvest of righteousness and peace for those who have been trained by it" (Heb. 12:11).

"Be careful to obey all the law my servant Moses gave you; do not turn from it to the right or to the left, that you may be successful wherever you go" (Josh. 1:7).

On the other hand, God takes seriously the rebellion of children against their parents. His warnings could not be more awesome, nor His judgment more severe.

"If a man has a stubborn and rebellious son who does not obey his father and mother and will not listen to them when they discipline him . . . Then all the men of his town shall stone him to death. You must purge the evil from among you . . ." (Deut. 21:18, 21).

"If a man curses his father or mother, his lamp will be snuffed out in pitch darkness" (Prov. 20:20).

"If anyone curses his father or mother, he must be put to death. He has cursed his father or his mother, and his blood will be on his own head" (Lev. 20:9).

The choice seems obvious. Who with the power of decision could possibly opt for bitterness, grief, ruin, and shame when instead they could have delight, peace, and respect? Yet many mothers are unwittingly choosing bad for themselves and their children daily as they allow their children to remain uncontrolled.

The Problem of Unrecognized Rebellion

Often this comes because parents do not recognize rebellion when they see it in its premature stages. During the course of the motherhood class, we compile a list of typical behavior displayed by undisciplined children. The list has included: saying no, directly disobeying, whining, incessant talking, running away from the parent, arguing with the parent, talking back, sassing, temper tantrums. In order to demonstrate the more subtle forms of disobedience, I play a tape recording that contains the following monologue. In it we find a mother visiting a friend in order to plan a meeting together. Instead of *telling* the daughter how she is expected to act and then requiring it of her, the mother tries to *persuade* her daughter to cooperate, with predictable results.

Oh, hi there, Jane. Sorry I'm late. I couldn't get a sitter, so I brought little Susie along. She promised she'd be as good as gold—didn't you, honey? She's just going to sit down here. . . . No, Susie, come over here by mother and you can color on the coffee table right beside us while we work on our Sunday school lesson. What? . . . No, dear, I don't want you to go over there. Come over here by mommy. What? . . . No, I want you where I can see you. . . . What? Well, all right, but don't touch anything.

Well, now! Where do we begin? Coffee? I'd love some. I was in such a rush this morning, I didn't get my usual. . . . What, Susie? No, dear, you can't have any coffee! You know you never have coffee! No, no, Jane. Please don't bother. Susie is just fine. Well, all right, if it's no trouble. . . . There, Susie, doesn't that orange juice look good? What do you say? Say thank you, dear. . . . Susie, say thank you. . . . Susie, no. Leave the orange juice here on the coffee table. No, you can't take it in there with you. No, Susie! You promised mommy you would be a good girl. Go and color.

What? You went just before we left! . . . Oh, for Pete's sake! Jane, where is your bathroom? . . . Thanks. I'm sorry for all this delay. Susie, it's right through that door. . . . No, you go on by yourself; you don't need me. What? . . . Whisper louder, dear, I can't hear you. . . . Don't be silly! Nothing's going to get you. . . . Oh, well! Just one more minute, Jane. Excuse us. We'll be right back. . . .

There we are! Now let's see if we can't get some work done! Susie, no, don't go up the stairs. No, dear. Go color. Susie, I said don't go up those stairs. You don't go walking around people's houses without their permission. *Come back down here!* . . . Susie! . . . One . . . two. . . . Susie, you better get down here before I get to five! I mean it, Susie! One . . . two . . . you'd better hurry! Three . . . I mean it, Susie! Four . . . Okay, Susie, you asked for it. . . . There, that's better. Now go color like you promised mommy. What? Yes, you can have some of your orange juice. . . . No, mommy already told you you can't have coffee. What's the matter with you? You never have coffee! Drink your orange juice and be still. I said no. Susie, let go of my arm. You're going to spill mommy's coffee. Oh, look what you've done to the lady's pretty carpet!

Susie's mother made several mistakes which caused her daughter to appear to be a spoiled brat. The problem, though, was not with the child, but with the mother. We should not *ask* our children to promise us they'll be good; *we* tell *them* how they are going to act, or else! Susie's mother had not decided what behavior she desired from her daughter. She told Susie no five or six times and then changed her mind and let the child have her way. Susie seems to have learned that her mother says no before she thinks and often doesn't really mean it.

Jesus said a Christian's yes should mean yes and his no should mean no. Parents should say, "I don't know, I'll have to think about it," if that is what they mean. A child who knows he can get his parents to change their minds by disobeying or whining will certainly do so at every opportunity.

The real test of our effectiveness in discipline, then, is not whether we sound good, mean well, or think positively, but whether or not our children obey us. *All the sound, psychologically correct phrases and sweet smiles in the world will not keep people from noticing that our children do not do what we tell them to do.*

What to Do

If our children are already out of control we may not know how to begin disciplining them. It is usually more difficult to correct a bad situation than it is to prevent it. For those who have this problem, I suggest a four-step plan of attack.

First, *talk to the Lord about your problem.* Through prayer and meditation on Scriptures such as those above, become thoroughly convinced that it is God's will that your children be obedient to you. Your good intentions will fade unless you are doing this for the Lord, out of a desire to be pleasing to Him and to glorify Him in your family life. Admit your inability to be strong in discipline and ask God to make good on His promise to make His strength perfect through your weakness (2 Cor. 12:9).

Second, *cultivate "the look."* When some women tell children to do something, I know by the uncertain expressions on their faces that they do not really expect the children to mind them. Remember, a child tends to do what he thinks others expect him to do. When you give an order, your face should look as though you haven't the slightest doubt that the person you are speaking to will obey you—and obey you quickly. You must have "the look." Practice it in front of the mirror until you scare yourself.

"The look" starts at the eyes. When you are really good at it, you can be standing clear across a room and smiling at someone else, but still let your child know with one glance, whether toddler or teen-ager, that he had better shape up fast. The technique involves looking the child straight in the eyes in a meaningful, warning, and, if necessary, menacing manner, and holding his gaze until you are sure he has received your message.

Queen Elizabeth has "the look." On tour of Canada, Prince Edward watched a pretty young harpist so intently while she was playing that she became flustered and broke a string. After the concert was over, the prince went to the young lady and apologized. "When I saw the look on Mum's face," he explained, "I knew I'd better get to you before she got to me."

A friend told me that her neighbor was a Roman Catholic who kept a tight rein in her home. One day my friend heard the mother tell her son to do something. "Why?" the child asked. "*Because I am the QUEEN!*" the mother shouted back.

Many of us could use some royal bearing from time to time in our dealings with our children. When the Bible tells us to "rule our households" (1 Tim. 5:14 RSV), it certainly is referring to our relationships with our children and our activities as homemakers, and not to our attitudes toward our husbands! "Strength and dignity," says Proverbs 31, clothe the godly wife and mother.

The eyes, the set of the chin, the firmness of the mouth, and the determined tone of voice all convey the message to our children that we feel in control of the situation, whether we really do at first or not. When some people say, "Clean your room!" it sounds more like "Clean your room?" No queen ever gave a command that sounded like a question. Our children will find it easier to obey the Lord's admonition to honor their mothers if we learn how to take charge when the occasion demands it.

The third step in gaining control over your children involves *calling your children together and outlining with them the changes that are going to be made.* Sit them down in the living room or some other place used for special occasions and say something like this: "I have been thinking lately about our family and have come to realize that some things about our life together are not pleasing to God. I have been letting you get by with talking back to me and with disobeying me, and I have been wrong to do that. In the Bible God says that parents are to train their children to obey them and that children are to accept their parents' authority over them. God promises to bless us as a family if we follow these rules, and He says that judgment will come to us all if we ignore His rules. I want God to bless our family. So from now on, this is what is going to happen. . . ."

Then go on to outline *exactly* what you expect and intend. For example, you might say, "Whenever I tell you to do something, I will give you one warning in my regular tone of voice. I will not yell any more. From now on I mean it the first time I say it, so you had better listen carefully when I speak. If you don't mind me immediately, I will either spank you, or fine you, or take away some privilege. If you make a fuss about it, I will increase the punishment. This will be hard on all of us, but that doesn't matter. What matters is that I must, and you must, start doing what God tells us to do."

Engender the feeling that everyone is starting at this point with a clean slate. Pray together about the new direction you are taking, and ask God to forgive each child and you for the disobedience of the past. Encourage the children to ask the Lord to help them do better, or pray for each of them by name out loud. Do *not* have the children promise to be good. You are not trying to win them over; you are explaining how things are going to be whether they like it or not.

The fourth step is the hardest of all. That is to *do what you said you would do*. Your children may be so stunned that things will go along beautifully for a day or two, but the honeymoon will not last. Do not allow yourself to hope that you will get by without a testing, because youngsters always have to find out just how firm the limits are. Prepare yourself mentally and emotionally for the encounters.

In the meantime, praise individual children for the efforts at cooperation you observe. If they remember their chores the first day without being reminded, say, "I appreciate the way you are taking care of your responsibilities. It makes the day go much more smoothly." If you notice a reduction in the amount of bickering, say, "Thank you, Jimmy, for not continuing that argument. Jesus said peacemakers will be blessed."

However, when a child disobeys, you must do what you have said you would do. Otherwise, you have lied to your children, and you are not keeping faith with God, who requires parents to control their children. Children do not respect those who are weak, and if you do not follow through in discipline, your children will come to disdain you.

Peter learned that Jesus had "the look," for after Peter had denied the Lord three times, one look from the Savior was enough to send him out into the darkness, weeping bitterly. Peter knew that Jesus' gaze was backed up by all of His divine power and authority. Neither Peter nor we would love and obey Jesus as we do if He were not worthy of our allegiance.

Mothers must assume the power and authority over their children given to them by God if they want their children to love and obey them, also. When children sense that an adult knows how to lead, they relax and respond positively to the adult. If a mother does not back up her words with action when it is needed, neither "the look," nor yelling, nor threats, nor pleading will produce disciplined children. The mother who does not discipline not only loses control of her children, she loses their love and respect as well.

Making It Personal

1. How do your answers to the first and second questions from "Before you read on" compare with those mentioned in the chapter? _____

_____

_____

_____

2. What are some specific actions commonly observed in undisciplined children? _____

_____

_____

_____

_____

3. What are some of the reasons children do not obey mothers? _____

_____

_____

_____

4. List in separate columns, Harvest of Undisciplined Children and Harvest of Disciplined Children, looking up verses in the Bible for emphasis.

_____   _____

_____   _____

_____   _____

_____   _____

_____   _____

5. How seriously does God view the rebelliousness of children? _____

_____

_____

_____

6. What are the four steps to instituting proper discipline?

_____

_____

_____

7. Will your children love you more if you are lenient?

_____

_____

_____

8. Read Matthew 4:5–7. How do some parents "tempt God" in child rearing (as Jesus would have done if He had complied)? _____

_____

9. Which Scriptures in this chapter most strongly motivate you to be firm in discipline? _____

_____

_____

10. How can Galatians 6:9 and Philippians 4:13 encourage parents? _____

_____

11. How do children benefit when their behavior is pleasing? See Exodus 20:12; Luke 2:52. _____

_____

Before you read on. . . . How much time does it take to discipline children? / What forms of discipline work best for you? / Do you and your husband generally agree in matters of discipline? / What does diligent discipline express? Read Proverbs 3:12 and 13:24. / What does the obedience of children express? Read John 14:15. / If the demands of discipline get you down, what should you do? (Read Matthew 11:28; Galations 6:9; Hebrews 12:11-12.)

8

CORRECTIVE DISCIPLINE

Adam and Eve had it made. They lived in a perfect environment, one that met their every need. They delighted in their companionship with each other, with the animals, and with their heavenly Father. They had no irritating neighbors, no aches or pains, no crabgrass. They had been given perfect freedom—except for one thing: they were not to try to discern right from wrong by themselves. They were to take God's word for it when He said not to do something; they were to obey Him; they were not to eat from the tree of the knowledge of good and evil. God set them a perfect example. He warned them. He loved them. Nevertheless, Eve and Adam disobeyed.

Despite all a parent's good intentions and best efforts, children will still be disobedient. This should not surprise us. Do we always follow the Lord perfectly? Do we sometimes knowingly do things which are not pleasing to our Father? We do, and it is not rational to expect any better conduct from our children.

We cannot say, however, "Oh, well, I won't discipline my child because I'm not perfect either." God's response to Adam and Eve shows clearly that disobedience cannot be overlooked or shrugged off as unimportant.

A child who steals small items with impunity will probably graduate to bigger things. An adolescent who gets by with coming home a few minutes later than his deadline will not worry about an even longer amount of time later. Also, if small infractions are allowed, how is anyone to know when the proper level of importance is reached? Such inconsistency is difficult for children to deal with. They can handle the certainty of discipline far better than they can the tension of wondering at what point the ax is going to fall. Inconsistent discipline makes children more bitter than dependable discipline.

Corrective measures, then, must be taken, which means even more work for parents. The mother and the father must be of one mind and in constant communication for best results. One of our teen-age sons got home twenty-one minutes past his curfew. The next day his father said, ''Was there any good reason for your being late last night?" Our son grinned sheepishly. "None that you'd think was too dandy, I suppose." So he was grounded for the next two nights.

This action seems cut and dried, but in real life questions do arise. I had a conference with my husband. Could our son go to a church meeting that might be called? Yes. Could he go to work if the manager called? Yes, but nowhere else.

Such understanding and support between parents is crucial. In our home we have a rule: Whatever answer you get from the first parent you ask is the answer you live with. If one of our children thinks his father would be more likely than I to let him or her do something, he or she is perfectly free to approach him, but he or she may never ask me if he says no, and vice versa. The child who does something because a second parent has said yes when the first parent has already said no is really in trouble! Such tactics are not tolerated.

Verbal Discipline

Probably the most common type of corrective discipline is *reproof*. Proverbs 29:15 says, "The rod and reproof give wisdom, but a child who gets his own way brings shame to his mother." Often verbal retraining—re-proof—is all that is necessary. Jesus reproved His disciples when they got off the track (Matt. 16:23). It comes rather naturally to say, "You shouldn't have done that. It was wrong. Don't do it again." But this should be followed by concrete advice. "If you are ever in that situation again, you must speak right up and say, 'I'm afraid it is my fault.'" With so much pressure to regard the most sinful acts as acceptable behavior, reproof is sorely needed in our world.

Physical Discipline

But there is no getting around the fact that the form of discipline most commonly referred to in the Bible is *spank-*

ing, or more scripturally, "beating with a rod" (Prov. 22:15; 23:13-14). Well-meaning psychologists have made this time-honored activity seem repugnant if not barbaric, but that is not the biblical view. We have been told that hitting our children teaches them to use physical force against their friends. Such an assertion is ridiculous. Spanking your child does not make him aggressive; it makes him obedient.

Spanking should not be considered a last resort. Especially with young children, spanking often best provides the immediate and powerful corrective needed.

Parents have also been told, "Never spank a child when you're angry." But Dr. Fitzhugh Dodson writes, "I think that is psychologically very poor advice. A child can understand when you strike him in anger. What a child cannot understand is when he disobeys his mother at 10:00 A.M., and she tells him, 'All right, young man, your father will deal with you when he gets home!'" Dr. Dodson advocates the "powwow" type of discipline: "your 'pow' followed by his 'Wow!'"[1]

Certainly parents should never let their exasperation overpower their judgment. "'In your anger, do not sin': Do not let the sun go down while you are still angry, and do not give the devil a foothold" (Eph. 4:26). Though it is possible to be angry without sinning, Satan would love for us to lose control. On the other hand, if I had waited until I cooled down before I spanked my children, I would seldom have given them the punishment they deserved: It is hard to spank when the emotion has died down. Besides, the tension the child experiences in waiting can be harder on him than the spanking.

The God of mercy and compassion warns us not to let feelings of pity prevent us from administering proper punishment (Deut. 7:16; 13:8-9; 19:13, 21). He tells us to have mercy on the poor and helpless and on those who repent and ask for forgiveness while there is still time. But Hebrews 12:17 informs us that Esau, when he finally realized what his sin was going to cost him, "found no place for repentance, though he sought for it with tears."

If it seems contradictory that we are told to love our children and then warned not to pity them so much that we do not punish their disobedience, perhaps it is because we do not recognize the *usefulness of pain.* Do you understand the meaning of pain in your life? Do you know what pain is for? Pain is the signal that something is wrong!

Several years ago I contracted a viral infection, commonly called shingles, in the nerve that services the right side of my face. The nerve was damaged as a result, so that I have little feeling on my right cheek and forehead. This usually does not bother me, but on several occasions I have burned myself with my curling iron without even realizing it, and have gone around for weeks with an unsightly scab on my face. A person who cannot feel pain is in danger. The numb part of his body could be burning, and he wouldn't know it until he smelled it! God forbid that any of us should never experience the warning of pain in our lives and then come before His judgment seat and learn for the first time all the wrong in our lives!

Correction is not meant to be fun. It is supposed to be distasteful enough to insure that the one on the receiving end never feels inclined to repeat the offense. A mother should be sure her tactics fulfill the scriptural assertion that "no discipline seems pleasant at the time, but painful" (Heb. 12:11).

God is love, and He administers discipline. Do not think you are being loving by withholding the pain of discipline from your children's lives. If we substitute the words "a mother" for the phrase "the Lord" in Hebrews 12:6, it would read, "A mother disciplines those she loves, and she punishes everyone she accepts as a son or daughter." God recommends spanking, not as the final recourse of a desperate parent, but as one of the normal ways to discipline our children.

Two Yellow Lights

However, there are one or two *cautions* that should be mentioned. The first is that, if experts are correct, children in every strata of society are being abused, and parents who abuse their children were probably themselves abused as children. Since Christians come from every kind of background, there are undoubtedly born-again believers who were abused as children. These parents may need special help in knowing how to discipline their children firmly but lovingly, in recognizing where spanking stops and abuse begins. They may feel uncontrollable rage welling up inside them in certain situations. I would entreat such mothers or fathers to get help from any hospital or mental health clinic, and to seek spiritual healing from the Lord and through His church. I would also beg them never to discipline their child if they cannot do it in a godly manner, but to leave such action to their spouses.

The second caution is my own opinion: when children are over the age of ten it is better to use other forms of discipline than spanking if at all possible. As children approach puberty, they become self-conscious about their bodies and react more positively to adult-like treatment. If parents feel strongly that the child should be spanked, they should seriously consider having the mother spank the girl and the father spank the boy. But it seems to me that other forms of discipline are not only more desirable but also more effective for older children because they do not humiliate the child in the process.

Unnecessary embarrassment only complicates an already emotion-charged disciplinary situation. Older boys may resent certain kinds of punishment when it is imposed by mothers. Perhaps this sort of consideration for our children's feelings is what the Bible means when it says, "Do not exasperate your children; instead, bring them up in the training and instruction of the Lord" (Eph. 6:4).

What other forms of discipline does a mother have at her disposal? What additional methods does the Bible suggest?

Natural Consequences

For the last several years, much has been said in educational circles about *logical* or *natural consequences*. This simply means allowing a person to learn from the natural results of his actions, and refraining from trying to protect him from the consequences of his own decisions. When our son broke his collarbone on the forbidden skateboard, the natural consequences of the pain and of missing his Little League championship game were punishment enough—you hardly spank a child with a broken collarbone.

Many women are overly protective of their children. They cannot bear for their children to have to learn from their mistakes. So the child learns that if he misses his bus through dawdling, his mother will drive him to school. If he spends his allowance foolishly, she will give him more money anyway. If he scratches the car, she will help him hide the fact from his father. If he continually forgets his lunch or school supplies at home, she will deliver them, and so on. Some women need to feel needed so badly and hope to win their children's love so desperately that they spend their lives trying to make up for the heedlessness of their offspring.

The end result is that the mother's time is considered to be of little value by the children, and they never learn to take responsibility for their own lives. The mother is teaching them to be undependable, slothful, and disorganized. She also is probably nagging them constantly about the very behavior she allows to continue.

The Bible recommends letting people learn, at times, from the natural consequences of their actions. In 2 Thessalonians

3:10 we find, "If a man will not work, he shall not eat." Deuteronomy 30:15-18 lays out God's general principle that life and prosperity come from obedience; death and adversity come from disobedience. Our children must learn this truth early if they are to develop godly characters.

Perhaps the most complete portrayal of natural consequences is found in the parable of the prodigal son (Luke 15:11-32). Surely the father would have preferred to prevent his son from wasting his share of the family fortune. But the son, it seems, like Adam and Eve, had to learn for himself. Notice, though, that the father, who represents God in the parable, although he watched anxiously for the son's return, did not go after his son. *He did not follow him and try to make everything work out painlessly.* Also, when the son finally returned, *he did not berate him: he allowed the experience to do the teaching.* Even more importantly, *he did not try to make it all up to his son.* The younger son's share was gone forever. The father makes this clear when he tells the older son, "Everything I have is yours" (v. 31).

Did it break the father's heart to know his son would suffer all his life from his sin? Probably—just as it would yours or mine. But to take more away from the older son in order to ease the lot of the younger would have been grossly unfair. How many times parents, out of love for an erring child, deprive more obedient children of their rightful share of time, interest, family resources, and emotional support! This harms the relationships of everyone in the family. Each child must learn to live prudently by judging beforehand whether an act will ultimately benefit him or not. Sometimes this kind of maturity can come only through painful experience.

We must emphasize, however, that natural consequences are not always a proper option for parents. We don't let a toddler learn the logical result of running out in front of a car, nor do we withhold a word of warning. But we do realize that there are times when letting a child learn from the results of his actions constitutes the most powerful corrective discipline there is.

Not all of God's consequences are "logical" to the natural man. We cannot know God's ways simply by deciding what would be logical to us. That is why we need the Bible and why we need to teach our children biblical principles. The world constantly tells us that pleasure and fulfillment will come by doing what seems the most fun at the moment. The prodigal son learned otherwise. May the Lord grant that our children will submit to His principles and avoid the hardship that comes with learning by sad experience.

Imposing Fines

The Bible mentions other forms of "artificial consequences" besides spanking. In His parable of the talents, Jesus has the master taking money away from the servant who did not manage it properly (Matt. 25:27-28). *Fining offenders* is commanded in Exodus 22:1-4 and other passages of Scripture. I'm almost embarrassed to admit that one of the reasons we started giving allowances to our young sons was so we would have something to take away as another disciplinary option. Losing money and what it can buy sobers most people very quickly.

Forfeiting Privileges

The *forfeiting of privileges* is another potent reminder for young people. It prepares them for living in a real world where, for example, a careless driver can have his license revoked. Esau, Reuben, Simeon, and Levi were denied the privilege of family leadership because of their sin; and children must learn that unwise or sinful actions can keep them from attaining some position or treat they want badly, also.

Taking away privileges is a less emotional form of discipline than spanking, a fact that adds to its appeal. "You can't play with your friends today because you did not clean your room yesterday as you were told. If you don't get it clean by five o'clock, you will be grounded again tomorrow." This kind of discipline moves most children to action while at the same time it allows the parent to remain calm and even friendly.

Isolating Offenders

Various scriptural references also suggest *isolating offenders* until they have repented of their deed. Young children often need nothing more than to be removed from an aggravating situation and given time to cool off. Their innate desire to be with people motivates them to shape up quickly. Whining, temper tantrums, and continual small squabbles can often be eliminated by putting the child by himself until he can display a change in behavior. He should not be allowed to rejoin the group while he is still sullen or irritable. A child who keeps on crying, for example, long after a spanking is over should either be spanked again for the temper he is exhibiting or isolated until he is completely over it and cheerful. Otherwise, he is still getting back at his parent for the discipline.

A mother should never allow a child to punish her for disciplining him by continuing negative behavior such as wailing, grouchiness, hitting her, or talking back. These responses show that the child is still rebelling and needs further discipline.

God requires more of young people than that they merely tolerate or even sulkily obey their parents. "Each of you must respect his mother and father. . . . I am the LORD your God" (Lev. 19:3). "Honor your father and your mother" (Exod. 20:12). God wants a positive response from children toward their parents. He requires not merely obedience, but cheerful obedience.

We desire for our children what God desired for Adam and Eve: that they should never have to experience sin for themselves but, through perfect obedience to their Father, they would do only right. We also know that in our fallen world and with our fallen natures this can never happen. Only Jesus lived a sinless life. Preventive discipline will not always be enough.

Since God has given us a record of the kinds of corrective discipline He endorses, He will also give us the wisdom to know which method to employ in a given situation. "Not that we are competent to claim anything for ourselves, but our competence comes from God" (2 Cor. 3:5).

Making It Personal

1. Does a perfect environment and perfect parenting insure perfect children? _____

_____

_____

_____

2. How important is agreement between parents in discipline? _____

_____

_____

_____

3. What are six forms of corrective discipline (be sure to include the biblical basis for each technique)? _____

_____

_____

_____

4. Is sulky obedience acceptable? _____

_____

_____

_____

5. What can we do when we lack wisdom in discipline? (See 2 Corinthians 3:5 and James 1:5.) _____

_____

_____

_____

6. Read *A Mother's Paraphrase of 1 Corinthians 13* on the next page. Does it give you any new insights?

_____

_____

_____

7. How can the following help a mother to deal properly with anger in disciplining her children: Ephesians 4:26; James 1:20; Hebrews 12:9, 11? _____

_____

_____

8. What cautions do you find in the following verses that can be applied to disciplinary situations: Proverbs 12:18; 17:27; James 1:26; Ephesians 4:29? _____

_____

_____

A Mother's Paraphrase of 1 Corinthians 13

Though I speak with the tones of the sweetest of angels and do not discipline, I am as effective as a wind chime or a babbling brook. And if I have much intelligence and understand great mysteries and all knowledge, and if I have all faith, so as to remove mountains, but do not discipline my children, they will gain nothing. If I give my children everything, sacrificing all my time and energies to provide them with whatever their hearts desire, but do not discipline, they will treasure nothing.

Discipline requires patience and kindness. Discipline is neither selfish nor simply power-hungry; it is not arrogant or rude. In discipline, a mother insists not on her *own* way, but on bringing her child in line with *God's* way; she is not irritable, nor does she carry grudges toward her children; she does not rejoice in wrong behavior but rejoices in the right. Discipline hopes all things, believes all things will work out for her child's good, bears and endures all that is required to bring these hopes to fulfillment.

Discipline never ends. As for a mother's words, they will become life-long echoes. As for her faith, it will, by God's grace, be mirrored in the child's own faith in Jesus Christ; her actions, vital memories. Her knowledge is imperfect and her discipline is imperfect. But when the perfect discipline of God comes into a child's life, the imperfect will pass away.

When they are children, they speak like children, they think like children, they reason like children, but when they grow up, they must put away childish things. For in our discipline they see through a glass darkly, but then, they will see Jesus face to face. Now they understand in part, but when they grow up into God's perfect discipline, they will know how kind our intentions were toward them, even as fully as we know these children whom we love.

Before you read on. . . . What do you feel is
the purpose of discipline? What should it accomplish? / How would you define self-
discipline? / How is self-discipline acquired?
/ How long do you feel children should be
under their parents' discipline?

9

THE PURPOSE OF DISCIPLINE

There is probably not a mother on earth who has not
thrown up her hands at the end of a particularly trying day
with her children and asked, "Why am I going through all
this? Why don't I just let them run wild like so many other kids

I see? Why make all this work for myself? Why not just hide behind my magazine and let them finish each other off?"

Of course the biggest reason we keep at the task of discipline is because the Lord requires it of us. That is why we plug away at every Christian work when the going gets tough. We do what we do because it is for the Lord, not because we feel like it or because it is convenient.

But it will also help us in our times of discouragement if we understand our goal in discipline. The purpose of discipline is *to form Christian character* in our children. In 1 Timothy 1:5, Paul states, "The goal of our instruction is love from a pure heart and a good conscience and a sincere faith" (NASB). We are trying to guard the hearts and consciences of our children during their early years so that they will not have to carry a heavy load of guilt about things they have done or the way they have treated others; and we are trying to engender a desire for love, purity, and sincerity within them.

The role of the parent is much like the law of the Hebrew people for the thousands of years until Christ came. In Galations 3:23-25, Paul teaches:

> But before faith came, we were kept in custody under the law. . . . Therefore the Law has become our tutor [child-conductor] to lead us to Christ. . . . But now that faith has come, we are no longer under a tutor [child-conductor] (NASB).

Parents, then, are to their children what the law was to God's people—their custodian, schoolmaster, and trainer—so that when the day of grace comes, when these children are out from under the authority of their parents, they will not depart from God's ways because they have been properly schooled. As it says in Hebrews 12, discipline "later . . . produces a harvest of righteousness and peace for those who have been trained by it" (v. 11).

My dictionary defines discipline as: "1) Training intended to produce a specified character or pattern of behavior,

2) Controlled behavior resulting from such training." So one goal of discipline is teaching our child desired character traits, and a second goal is to have one of those desired traits, self-discipline, sufficiently formed to carry the child through the rest of his life. Godly character persists only if parental discipline is replaced by self-discipline. For there is a time when a young person thinks, acts, and talks as a child, but as he becomes older, he must put away childish things.

Self-discipline is, to a large degree, a matter of habits of conduct acquired by imposed discipline. But one major aspect of self-discipline is the agreement of the individual involved that the conduct is correct and benefits him in some basic, important way.

The military life is extremely disciplined. But how much of that imposed conduct carries over into everyday life after discharge, or how many elect to remain in the military? Do ex-servicemen continue to rise while it is still dark, make their beds carefully, shine their shoes to mirror brightness, and keep the creases in their clothes? They do so only if they themselves have seen the value of such actions.

What we are striving for, then, is not only to bring our children in line with what we believe or know is best for them, but also to do it in such a way that they will see for themselves the benefits of godly behavior so that the habits will carry over into their adult lives. Then, and only then, will they be able and willing to use those ingrained principles when they have to make judgments in situations they have not faced before.

We have all seen children who are models of good behavior when with a demanding parent but who lose control when away from the parent, for instance, playing with other children or at school. The reverse is also true. Some children run all over their parents but shape up immediately in the presence of a teacher or other adult. These children are still under the law rather than grace in that they have not learned *self-*control but need continually to have discipline enforced from the outside. Such a child is nervous and unhappy because his personality is not integrated. He becomes different people at different times. He must always be looking over his shoulder to see if the authority figure is there so he knows which personality to exhibit.

In Galations 5:22-23 we find self-control listed as part of the fruit of the Spirit. This means that true self-discipline or self-control grows only where the Holy Spirit is in charge. Our human efforts, no matter how sincere or prayerful, can take our children only so far. They will not have the power to live the life of freedom from the law of parental discipline in a manner pleasing to God until they have come to a personal faith in Christ and the Holy Spirit dwells within them.

The fruit of the Spirit also includes love, joy, peace, patience, kindness, goodness, faithfulness, and gentleness, which can be thought of as part of the Christian character we as parents hope to see produced in our children. Our discipline is meant to keep our children on the right track until they receive Jesus Christ as their Savior and Lord. This step of faith is the crucial step, not only for salvation, but for personal maturity. It is a person's faith in Christ that opens his eyes to the benefits of the disciplined life and empowers him to live it when parental discipline is gone. Any lesser resolve or motivation is insufficient to weather the pressures and temptations of life.

Just as parents should grasp every opportunity to teach their children God's ways, so must they continually pray for and provide opportunities for their children to make a personal commitment of their lives to Jesus Christ. Even after young people receive Christ, they still have much to learn, and parental instruction continues until they are ready to strike out on their own. It is important for us, then, to make not only the substance of our discipline, but the principles involved, clear and valuable to our children so that when they are free from our direct control they will know how to handle their freedom.

Children are not supposed to remain dependent on their parents forever. They must be equipped to face victoriously the challenges of the world, and we must see to it that they do not attain independence lacking the skills and knowledge necessary for success. Paul concludes his discussion on law and grace with a warning which godly parents cannot help but echo for their children: "You . . . were called to be free. But do not use your freedom to indulge the sinful nature" (Gal. 5:13).

Making It Personal

1. What is the purpose of discipline? _____

_____

_____

_____

2. Compare law and grace, and parent control and independence. Use scriptural references. _____

_____

_____

_____

3. How far can parental control take children? What must children do to complete their own maturity? _____

_____

_____

_____

4. What is the internal motivation that changes a person from mere outward conformity to whole-hearted discipline? (Col. 3:22-24.) _____

_____

5. What can a parent do to prepare a teenager for going off to college or living on their own? _____

_____

_____

6. Where does the power for consistent self-control and other positive character traits come from (Gal. 5:16–25)? _____

_____

_____

7. What means can we expect God to use to bring about spiritual strength in our children as well as ourselves (James 1:2–4)? _____

_____

_____

Before you read on. . . . What traits do you feel are most important for your child to possess? How are you helping to build these into their lives? / What traits do you want *not* to see in your children? How are you guarding against these negative traits? / How should a mother judge her children? Read 1 Samuel 16:7. / How is character formed? Read Romans 5:3-4. / What are the most prominent character traits—both good and bad—of each of your children?

10

CHRISTIAN CHARACTER AND PERSONALITY

Peter Marshall used to say that the trouble with preachers is that they too often aim at nothing and hit it. Unfortunately, this can also be said of many parents with regard to their children's characters. Although there are scores of character traits mentioned in the Bible, most of us would be hard put to list more than a handful. This presents a serious problem: How can we encourage our children to develop positive character traits if we do not know what they are?

Even Christians cannot trust that their children will just naturally develop sterling characters because of their parents' spiritual insights, for the Bible reveals that spiritual people often have reared ungodly offspring. Eli, the priest who foretold the birth of Samuel, had sons who, though priests themselves, were totally corrupt. "Eli's sons were wicked men; they had no regard for the LORD. . . . the sin of the young men was very great in the LORD's sight, for they were treating the LORD's offering with contempt" (1 Sam. 2:12, 17).

Jacob also produced sons who had serious moral flaws. Jacob's own analysis of their characters in Genesis 49 makes clear why he felt it necessary to pass over his three oldest sons and elect Judah, the fourth born, as leader of the family. Reuben was "unstable as water" (v. 4 RSV); Simeon and Levi were rejected because of their cruel and wanton anger.

David's son Adonijah was a handsome, proud, and arrogant young man who raised himself up as king while his father still sat on the throne. The Bible tells us that David "had never interfered with him by asking, 'Why do you behave as you do?'" (1 Kings 1:6).

Christian parents must inquire into the conduct of their children, for "even a child is known by his actions, by whether his conduct is pure and right" (Prov. 20:11). This does not mean that we panic at the wayward actions of a two-year-old, but it does mean that we take seriously any developing patterns our children may display in their childhood years and endeavor to take corrective measures before certain tendencies become fixed parts of their characters.

We also need to make a clear distinction between what I would call "personality traits" and "character traits." For our purposes, I would like to refer to "personality traits" as those characteristics which, of themselves, carry little or no moral weight and are acceptable as a part of a Christian's personality. "Character traits," however, will be those characteristics that are taught biblically as being right or wrong for a Christian. The list below will give some examples of the kinds of distinctions I am drawing.

Personality Traits

introvert	—	extrovert
enjoys working with hands	—	prefers mental projects
higher intelligence	—	lower intelligence
serious	—	whimsical
gregarious	—	prefers solitude
marked sense of humor	—	little sense of humor
enjoys fantasy	—	realistic
idealistic	—	pragmatic
sensitive to moods	—	not sensitive to moods
emotions spontaneous	—	emotions controlled
enjoys eating	—	food unimportant
physically coordinated	—	physically uncoordinated
verbalizes easily	—	less verbal
meticulous	—	casual
self-motivated	—	externally motivated
methodical	—	unorganized
artistic	—	unartistic
musical	—	nonmusical

As we look over this partial listing, we will undoubtedly find some traits that we would prefer for our child to display and others that we would hope he would not. But these are not the most important areas for a parent to evaluate. Whether a person is physically adept or not may make a great difference in the direction of his life as far as his occupation and leisure-time activities are concerned, but this should not be of primary concern to his parents. For God is far more concerned about our inner lives than He is in our surface characteristics.

Personality can express character, but it can also disguise character for awhile. That is why it is important for people to know each other for a long time before contemplating marriage or business partnerships with them. Character cannot be hidden forever, but will be revealed sooner or later; and mothers, who have the opportunity to observe their children in every type of situation, have the responsibility to use these occasions to perceive their youngsters' true characters.

The Bible warns us about assessing people in a superficial manner. When Samuel was sent to anoint the new king, he was told, "Do not consider his appearance or his height. . . . The LORD does not look at the things man looks at. Man looks at the outward appearance, but the LORD looks at the heart" (1 Sam. 16:7). Godly mothers must follow God's instructions in this area as well.

Many biblical character traits could be listed. Perhaps a worthwhile subject for family devotions would be to search together for characteristics to add to the list below.

Character Traits

honest	—	deceitful
truthful	—	untruthful
self-controlled	—	uncontrolled
loyal	—	disloyal
diligent	—	neglectful
obedient	—	disobedient
dependable	—	undependable
humble	—	proud
patient	—	impatient
peaceful	—	irritable
considerate	—	self-centered
prudent	—	foolish
gentle	—	harsh

content	—	envious, covetous
kind	—	unkind
modest	—	boastful
pure	—	impure
respectful	—	disrespectful
meek	—	self-willed
spiritual	—	carnal
forgiving	—	spiteful
appreciative	—	ungrateful
generous	—	stingy, selfish

The Bible says young John the Baptist "grew and became strong in spirit" (Luke 1:80). Of Jesus, we read, "And the child grew and became strong; he was filled with wisdom, and the grace of God was upon him" (2:40). Not one word about how well they did in Little League, or how popular they were on the block, or how they kept wearing holes in the knees of their jeans!

However, as mothers we often spend more time worrying about our children's social standing or health habits than their characters. We sometimes take more pride in what our children can *do* than in what they *are*. We expend more energy thinking about what they are going to do for a living when they grow up than we do about what kind of a person they are going to *be* when they grow up. We make more of an effort to change their personalities, which have little moral importance, than we do to guide their characters, in which God is most interested.

There are thousands of honorable life vocations for our children; and some that will be most needed when our children reach adulthood are not even known now—who had heard of computer technicians when we were young? Mothers waste much energy and emotion worrying about things in the future instead of investing their time in the present. For the truth is that a child who has learned honesty, patience, trustworthiness, and such is likely to succeed at whatever he or she decides to pursue; while gifted individuals with faulty characters may not be able to capitalize on their potential.

How, then, do we go about encouraging the character traits we so desire? First of all, we model them in our own lives. The mother who tells her child there aren't any cookies instead of saying truthfully, "Yes, there are some, but you may not have any," is teaching her child to lie. Parents who allow their teenagers to pay the price for younger children at the movie theater are teaching their children to lie and cheat. They are as much as saying, "If you can't afford to get something honestly, don't do without it—get it any way you can."

Those who ridicule political leaders or schoolteachers at home are giving their offspring a lesson on how to be disrespectful; and parents who make fun of those of other races or backgrounds are showing their children how to be unloving. Parents who do not perform their tasks faithfully and cheerfully, whether these commitments are to church, community, or home life, are teaching their children to be undependable and sullen.

Children are fantastically quick to pick up the smallest inconsistencies in parental standards. When a mother lets her child eat grapes before they are paid for in a store or does not give back money when she has received too much change—each of these supposedly minor incidents is stored in a child's computer and used when the occasion calls for it. If she insists that her children stop sucking their thumbs or give up their favorite blanket, but protests that she can't quit smoking or lose some of her extra twenty pounds, the double standard will not go unrecognized for long. If she does not follow through on discipline, her children know it.

In addition, mothers must verbalize their standards, as well as model them, so the child will relate the principle to the act.

There are times when you will have to explain to your child in a calm, respectful way that some leader or teacher or relative was not right to do something, and explain the principle involved. The child can learn to respect the office while analyzing the actions of the person who fills the office if you do so yourself.

This all takes time. It takes consistency. It takes emotional energy. It takes constant references to the Scriptures. It takes prayer for discernment. It takes patience, diligence, gentleness—do you see? *The demands on your own character* in the building of your children's characters are *enormous.* Those who decide not to have any children are precluding one of God's most effective ways of forcing us to grow up.

In order to master motherhood, then, we will have to continue the daily fight to master our own reactions and emotions, to bring our own personalities and characters more in line with Christ's perfect character.

Our children learn more from us than from any other source. Is it this tremendous pressure that makes some mothers want to avoid their calling as mothers? Possibly. Like Jonah, we may try to run away from our God-appointed task and deny its claim on us. But God still holds us responsible, and, like the prophet, we run away to our peril.

Making It Personal

1. What warning do you find in the lives of Eli, Jacob, and David? _____

_____

_____

_____

_____

_____

102 • *Mastering Motherhood*

2. Is the distinction between personality traits and character traits helpful? What other traits could be added to either list?

_____

_____

_____

3. Do you give your child recognition more for personality traits that please you or for expressions of good character traits? _____

_____

_____

_____

4. Is your own character being conformed daily to the character of Christ? Read Romans 8:29. _____

_____

_____

_____

5. How can a mother encourage the growth of godly character traits in her children? _____

_____

_____

_____

6. Do you know your children? List the predominant personality and character traits, good and bad, of each of your children. _____

_____

_____

_____

Before you read on. . . . How much time do you spend each week: a) cleaning the house, doing laundry, meal preparation, mending, etc.? b) at work or at meetings? c) in activities with your children? d) talking on the telephone? e) watching TV or reading? / What effects could a consistently disorganized household have on the character of a child? / What is the primary role of every Christian, including mothers? Read Philippians 2:7 and Matthew 20:25-28. Is this a role of weakness or strength? In what specific way is this role carried out by women? Read Proverbs 31:13-24. / If you live to be seventy, how many years will you have left after your youngest child reaches the age of eighteen?

11

A MOTHER'S TIME

Many myths are commonly circulated about the plight of the modern housewife and mother, most with a basis in fact, but none completely true. Women of my acquaintance are not chained to their homes in an endless round of drudgery, though they do get tired of picking up the same toys and laundering the same clothes again and again. Neither are they addicted to the television and telephone, although some admit to having to limit both through an act of the will. Nor are they galavanting around town with carefree abandon. Rather, their away-from-home hours are generally absorbed by activities they would resign if they could conscientiously do so: employment, church and community commitments, family business.

The tensions most women seem to feel are those that stem from the complicated schedules our society encourages for every member of the family. They arise because of the prevailing conviction that all of us must develop and maintain all of our potential all of the time. We must, or so we feel, be at the peak of our physical, emotional, spiritual, charitable, mental, and economic perfection at any given moment. If not, we must remedy the lack through taking up the current fad sport or joining an exercise class; attending another Bible study; cutting, curling, or coloring our hair; going to real estate school; volunteering at the hospital; or taking sensitivity training. The list is endless.

Few of us understand how different our lives are from those of mothers fifty years ago. True, they may have made their own bread, washed clothes on a scrubboard, and ruined their nails coping without our labor-saving devices. But older women tell me there weren't nearly so many clothes to wash. Children had one or two outfits for school that were laundered once a week, and their Sunday clothes, which were seldom washed. No one wondered what to wear or noticed another's lack of wardrobe unless his only clothes were ragged or he had no "Sunday best." The washing and ironing were tiring, but the volume was certainly less.

If the family owned a car, the mother didn't drive it. No doubt it was inconvenient to have to walk at times, but groceries were delivered to the house, and no one expected you to attend six meetings across town every week or chauffeur your children anywhere. No one felt that a woman of forty had to look as though she were thirty, nor did they expect her to flush with embarrassment if she was forced to admit she didn't play a good game of tennis.

Today's life style has created new stresses, and mothers would do well to take a hard look at just how they are spending their time. Our culture must not control us. The expectations of our friends cannot be the determining factor in our decisions about the most beneficial way to conduct our lives.

The Bible has some practical suggestions to make that will help clarify our thinking. First of all, let us mention what we are *not* to do with our time.

> "Seldom set foot in your neighbor's house—too much of you, and he will hate you" (Prov. 25:17).
> ". . . they [women] get into the habit of being idle and going about from house to house. And not only do they become idlers, but also gossips and busybodies, saying things they ought not to" (1 Tim. 5:13).

Some women enjoy being with other people every possible minute, but this can be as detrimental to their personal fulfillment as being isolated from others all the time. Neither extreme is good. If we are not comfortable being alone at times, we should make it a matter for prayer or talk to a Christian counselor. Our fulfillment should not come from constant contact with people, but in our relationships with our Lord and our families. An overpowering need to visit with others, the Scriptures warn, will cause us to sin by neglecting our responsibilities, gossiping as we run out of other topics of conversation, meddling in others' affairs, and saying things we should not. When a woman openly discusses things about her husband that betrays confidences and invades his privacy, then it can no longer be said, "Her husband has full confidence in her. . . . She brings him good, not harm, all the days of her life" (Prov. 31:11-12).

Mothers do not lack for advice on how to spend their time—each of us could fill our days ten times over. But God has some specific things for us to accomplish, and our sense of satisfaction at a day's end depends on how closely we come to completing *His* plans for that day. "Train the young women to love their husbands and children, to be sensible, chaste, domestic, kind, and submissive to their husbands, so that the word of God will not be discredited" (Titus 2:4-5 RSV). "These commandments that I give you today are to be upon your hearts. Impress them on your children. Talk about them when you sit at home and when you walk along the road, when you lie down and when you get up" (Deut. 6:6-7).

Proverbs 31 alone contains enough suggestions to keep a mother fully occupied. "She selects wool and flax and works with eager hands. She . . . bring[s] her food from afar. She gets up while it is still dark; she provides food for her family. . . . She considers a field and buys it; out of her earnings she plants a vineyard. . . . She opens her arms to the poor. . . . She makes coverings for her bed. . . . She makes linen garments and sells them, and supplies the merchants with sashes. . . . She speaks with wisdom, and faithful instruction is on her tongue. She watches over the affairs of her household and does not eat the bread of idleness." The woman is nothing if not industrious!

What kinds of things is she busy doing, this woman who is called an "excellent wife"? She is doing those very things Titus mentioned centuries later and Moses mentioned centuries earlier. She is being sensible, chaste, domestic, kind, subject to her husband; and she is teaching and caring for her children.

Domestic. The word is often used to refer to someone hired to do the most menial tasks. But that is not the connotation intended in the Bible. To be *domestic* means to be "fond of things pertaining to the family or home"; and despite all the cultural pressure to the contrary, a woman's primary calling from God is "to love her husband and children, to be . . . domestic."

I have heard many women talk about how they can hardly wait to get their children in school, as if at that magic age mothers can pat themselves on the back for a job well done and spend the rest of their lives focusing on their own self-fulfillment. Dr. Saul Brown, director of psychiatry at Cedars-Sinai Medical Center in Los Angeles, says "There is a tendency in society to turn kids over to someone else, sometimes for economic reasons because both parents must work, sometimes because the parents want to do their own thing. We are moving to the danger point of children not finding reassurances that they have deep value to their parents."[1]

When mothers work full time outside the home they are depriving their children in some important areas. Honesty demands that we face up to this fact. If a mother's work puts food in her children's mouths that would not be there otherwise, then her job is a necessity; but it does not change the truth that her children are at the same time being denied much personal and emotional satisfaction by her absence from the home.

For the first time in our nation's history, more women are now working outside the home than are staying at home. I have found that each mother feels that her situation is unique, that her inner needs or the extra money desired makes her decision to vacate the home all right, when in fact these statistics show working mothers to be in the majority. Recent studies reveal that *41 percent* of United States mothers with *children under age six work outside the home*. These mothers account for about six million children. In addition, millions of school-age children across this nation come home from school to empty houses every day.

Perhaps the problem has been stated most personally and touchingly by a New England businessman writing under a pen name (for obvious reasons) in the *American Home* magazine. Although written about a woman who had pre-schoolers at home, its truths could apply to women who have children of any age.

> My wife has been out working for a year and I wish she were home raising our children. I can't tell her that. I can't tell anyone. I can't say anything so disloyal, outrageous, and reactionary. All of her friends are working mothers. Everyone would think I was against the women's movement, against independence and free expression for women. . . .
>
> It is not something I can discuss with her. You see, there is no rational basis for her role change. She earns $14,000; the housekeeper gets $10,000. Obviously, my wife is not working for money. She has an entry-level management job with a large company. It isn't particularly rewarding, but she believes it will lead somewhere. Whether or not it will is not the point, either. The reason she is working is that it isn't acceptable in terms of her self-esteem for her not to work. She and the friends she respects (all of her "role models") have been conditioned by the media to believe that there is no life without a job. In other words, a job is an end in itself. This has become the trendy party line of the magazines, books, and television writers of the '70's. Climb on the bandwagon, ladies. You have no choice.
>
> My wife didn't feel that *she* had a choice. She didn't even consider that she was giving up the full-time job of mothering for which she is well qualified by temperament and background for the other full-time job. She didn't weigh in the balance the effect of withholding her love, knowledge, and guidance from her children in their formative years.

Don't tell me quality is better than quantity. That's what she told me. It goes this way: It's not the amount of time you devote to your children but the degree of giving that takes place during that time. That's another specious hype invented by writers who have never lived through the situation. What happens in real life is that my wife comes home from work tired and grumpy. She snaps at the children. The quality of that time is awful. Weekends are better, but that is also when we play tennis and entertain friends, run errands, and spend time with each other. In other words, the quality is better then, but the quantity is so limited that I wonder if that sparse, part-time parenting makes up for all the lost time.

I think my wife feels guilty about the situation, too, and that tends to make her more frazzled. Her formerly sunny nature seems to be eclipsed for longer and longer periods of time.

Can a father be substituted for the mother in this equation? Theoretically yes, but in our real-life drama, no. I can't stay at home with the children and do my work, and we need the income from my work to live. . . .

I guess I feel guilty, too. After all, I got all of us used to our present standard of living, and I certainly don't want to make a change in it. I have read all the psychology books about the importance of the early years in child development, but I have also known children of two-job families who grew up all right and children whose mothers stayed home and grew up with problems. So why am I worried?

We will both have our careers and the children will grow up very nicely and we will all live happily ever after. But I didn't write the script. I'm not even the director. I'm just one of the actors in this real-life movie. I am only playing the role assigned to me by society. And my wife is playing hers. I wish I believed in the happy ending they've written for us.[2]

In Greek mythology, many sailors were lured to their destruction by the singing of Siren, a sea nymph. The sound of her beautiful voice drew them too close to the rocks, and their ships were dashed into pieces. Mothers are too often enticed by the "Siren songs" of materialism and self-fulfillment. The Scriptures warn about the dangers of falling in love with worldly goods and of letting the culture squeeze us into its mold (Rom. 12:2). Let us instead hear the sound of the siren as we regard it today—as a signal or warning device alerting us to danger.

Is the idea of sacrificing for our children passé? Couldn't a family get along financially if the mother stayed home and saved money by serving fewer convenience foods, buying no clothes for her job, having fewer transportation expenses, and hiring fewer babysitters? Is an expensive home without a mother of more value than a modest one occupied by her?

Perhaps it is time for women to begin lobbying for more part-time jobs. Churches and businesses could easily have several half-time secretaries instead of a few full-time ones. Women could teach three periods a day instead of carrying a full load. In one school district, I was hired to teach half a day at half salary while an "intern" from the state college taught the remaining hours. Substitute teachers and emergency secretarial service employees can limit the number of days they work. Some people who travel to their jobs could just as easily do them at home. However, even part-time employment at home (such as writing) can leave you tired and irritable.

If you absolutely must work full time, then the Lord knows that, and you can trust Him to help you find a solution that will not harm your children. But to those who are simply caught in the tide of contemporary behavior, our Lord would bring a warning: "What good will it be for a man if he gains the whole world, yet forfeits his soul? Or what can a man give in exchange for his soul?" (Matt. 16:26). Perhaps women could personalize and paraphrase His words: What good will it be for a mother if she gains the whole world, yet forfeits her own children? Or what can a mother give in exchange for her children?

The worries of working mothers surface any time they are asked about their families. One woman said her husband had encouraged her to return to school "because for several years I made him miserable by asking what I should do with my life. I know that he is pleased with what I'm doing, and he and the children have been very supportive—by accepting the horrible meals.

"Sometimes I've asked myself, 'Is it worth it?' Our children have a lot more chores than other children, and they'll say, 'Well, so-and-so's mother does this and that,' and then I have that—not guilt—but almost sorrow. Am I giving enough to the kids? Every once in a while, I get a chill. Am I going to end up with screwed-up kids? I keep telling my children that when they get older and look back, they will be proud of me."

The trouble is, we won't know if our children are going to be "screwed-up" until it is too late. Nevertheless, record numbers of mothers are forging ahead with blind optimism, as if the terrible fate of many of today's families can never happen to them, gambling with stakes they can't afford to lose.

Studies affirm, however, that more employed married women have extramarital affairs than do homemakers. Teenage alcoholism and drug use is at a record high as young people fill up their free hours any way they can. Instances of teen-age girls running brothels in their parentless homes after school or while truant are not uncommon.

Children are not the only ones who can be neglected when a mother's energies are drained by outside employment. Husbands often get short shrift, not the loving consideration the Lord desires. In addition, women are urged in 1 Timothy 5:10 not only to devote themselves to "bringing up children," but also to "showing hospitality, . . . helping those in trouble and devoting herself to all kinds of good deeds." A woman who already is trying to juggle the demands of two full-time jobs—one in the home and one outside of it—seldom has time to expend on the poor or needy.

Bible study and prayer, requirements for all believers, also tend to suffer. Fellowship with other Christians and church attendance and participation can become resented obligations instead of joys. More than one mother has told me that she has seen her husband and children off to church but stayed home herself in order to have some time alone! If she were not working, she could have arranged time for herself while the children were at school without taking the Lord's time to do it. Unspiritual attitudes of all kinds tend to surface whenever a person is tired, under pressure, or faced with more then can reasonably be accomplished, and a working mother is usually all of these.

Of course, a mother can be home every day without being the least "domestic"—without exhibiting any love for home and family. Her house can be in a shambles, her children ignored. Her spiritual life and her husband can be more neglected than those of career women. The Bible makes it plain that this kind of woman is not obeying God's purpose for her. If she has "housewife's depression," it is not because she is at home; it is because she is not doing at home those things that will bring her fulfillment. Jesus came that we might have life and have it more abundantly. As it did for Paul, happiness will come to us as we learn to be content with the life God has assigned to us.

If a woman does not work outside the home, it really does not require continuous, back-breaking labor to keep a house in decent condition. I know from personal experience that it takes two or three weeks of neglect before bathrooms look like the gas station rest rooms in the middle of the New Mexico desert. A woman whose home is obviously out of control has been shirking her responsibilities for a very long time. She is not doing her housework "as unto the Lord." Her family, her friends who visit, her Lord, and her own self-esteem deserve better than she is giving. She is letting other activities or idleness keep her from being the kind of homemaker God admires in Proverbs 31.

Mothers who are at home all day should see to it that their children benefit from that fact. Does mom make it a point to pause in her labors when her youngsters walk in from school and spend a few minutes in conversation with them, or does she continue talking on the telephone without even a friendly nod? Does she try to arrange it so she can sometimes work alongside a child, or does she always send him off to complete the task alone? Do her children know they have priority over her other interests? Do they come home to find their mother has done for them what she promised to do, or that she forgot?

Mothers who choose to devote themselves to their families should personally benefit from their decision also by having some time for themselves, and no discussion of a mother's time would be complete without emphasizing the legitimacy of this need. When God set aside the seventh day as a day of rest, He established the principle that everyone needs to get away from the daily grind.

Most women agree heartily with such sentiments but find that with young children at home their attempts to get away often end in failure, leaving them frustrated. Their courses of action are limited. A mother can:

1) exchange babysitting with a friend; but this leaves her paying for her free time by caring for her friend's children. Sometimes it is not worth it to work twice as hard when you have to return the favor, especially if the friend's children are hard to control.

2) have her husband take over. If he is willing to cooperate and spend part of his day off this way, it can work beautifully. However, many women complain that

when they come home they find the house strewn with toys and are faced with assorted problems because fathers often do not *work* at babysitting. Men tend to feel that *being* there is enough and don't pay attention to what junior is up to until it is too late.

3) hire a responsible person during the day to watch her children. This kind of expense is often prohibitive for the young mothers who need it the most, and it is not always possible to find college girls or women who are interested in this type of work.

Each solution has its drawbacks, and a woman should try to find the one that works best for her, the one that leaves her with the fewest worries and irritations in exchange for her precious free hours.

A woman can expend a lot of money, planning, and energy, however, only to find she has received no re-creation at all. It is a wise mother indeed who knows herself well enough to know what activity will really bring her the relaxation she needs. Many women crave physical outlets such as tennis, golf, or swimming in order not to feel hemmed in by life, while others need to express themselves through art or music.

Sometimes it is not that the mother needs to get out of the house; it is more that she needs to have someone *take the children away* for a period of time so she can have the house all to herself. This, I have found over the years, has often been the most restoring time of all; and husbands are often better at watching the kids at a park or a movie than at home. It can be a real joy to lock the doors, take the telephone off the hook, and just listen to the silence! I can even enjoy cleaning house when the house is empty; and reading, or sipping a cup of coffee, or making a dress when I am all alone can bring more peace than many things which I have to leave the house to do.

Whatever the activity, Jesus' words to mothers are the same as those to the disciples: "Come with me by yourselves to a quiet place and get some rest" (Mark 6:31). The Shepherd would still lead His sheep beside the still waters and make them lie down; He knows our souls need restoring.

Mothers need to make their leisure time a matter for prayer so that the Lord can reveal to them what will really meet their needs and they can have the assurance that He will bless their efforts. If our free time is placed in the Lord's hand, then delays, sick children, and broken plans can be accepted as part of His will.

If all this sounds as though I have struggled personally with the problem of getting time for myself, it is because I have. I have had at least one preschooler at home for fifteen out of the last nineteen years, and had three preschool sons at one time. In addition, my husband's office was in our home for seven of those years. When our last child started staying at school until two o'clock in the afternoon and my husband's office moved out permanently, our two older sons were attending a local community college and were often home during the day at odd hours (they worked in the evenings), so that my times of real privacy remained limited.

Since I am a person who enjoys solitude, this has at times been a spiritual problem for me, and as with many of life's pressures, the real questions were: Is God in control of my life? Do all things really work together for my good (Rom. 8:28)?

My problem may not seem overwhelming to others, but I have found that it is sometimes easier to trust God in the obvious crises of life than it is in the day-to-day routine irritations that arise. Such unresolved resentments produce "housewife's depression" and bad feelings toward family members.

A mother must learn to trust God for free time as she trusts

Him for everything else. Prayer for time alone, as all other prayers, can be answered either yes, no, or wait. Our ideas about what we need are not always correct, but the Lord's are. He will, as the Good Shepherd, take care of our every need.

We need to pray not only for our leisure time, but to consider prayerfully what the Lord might like to change about the way we spend the rest of our time, also. As with His sheep whom He calls by name (John 10:27), He has a daily plan for us, a path or a pasture prepared for us (Ps. 23). Some of us need to work harder at cleaning house; others of us need to stop worrying so much about keeping everything overly neat and spend more time playing with our children. Some may need to join a group for Bible study and prayer; others may need to quit volunteering for everything and pamper their husbands instead. We may need to lose weight, or plan more healthful meals, or stop wasting time watching TV, or improve our grooming, or volunteer to help in our child's room at school, or get off by ourselves for awhile and be completely alone.

Whatever it is that God would want for us, may our response be that of the psalmist:

> But I trust in you, O LORD;
> I say, "You are my God."
> My times are in your hands" (Ps. 31:14-15).

Making It Personal

1. How are the pressures on women today different from those of fifty years ago? _____

_____

_____

_____

2. Who or what determines how you personally spend your time? _____

_____

_____

_____

3. How much time should women spend visiting one another? What are the dangers of coffee klatsches? _____

_____

_____

_____

4. List the things God wants a woman to do with her time.

_____

_____

_____

_____

5. What does it mean to be "domestic"? _____

_____

_____

_____

_____

6. If you felt God was saying to you personally, "Quit your job!" would you do it? _____

_____

_____

_____

_____

7. If you felt God was saying to you personally, "Glorify Me in your housekeeping," what changes would you have to make? _____

_____

_____

_____

8. How do you make time for yourself? (See Mark 6:31.)

_____

_____

_____

9. How is Romans 8:28 true for mothers? _____

_____

_____

_____

10. What does Psalm 31:14-15 mean to you? _____

_____

_____

_____

11. Identify and commit areas of personal need to the Lord.

_____

_____

_____

Before you read on. . . . Do you feel good about yourself as a person? / Do you praise your children for positive actions? / How many minutes per day do you spend in conversation with your children? / Does your child's teacher at school make him feel like a worthwhile person? / Do the children in your family "put each other down"? / Have you ever "played to your audience" while disciplining—that is, doing what those who were watching you would approve of?

12

BUILDING SELF-ESTEEM IN CHILDREN

Self-esteem, feeling good about oneself, is perhaps the most easily destroyed aspect of the human personality. All of us feel insecure or inadequate in some areas of our lives, but there are those who face each day full of fear and anxiety because they never learned to value themselves and feel that they are not worth much.

Everyone reading this has an opinion of herself and her worth, an opinion based mainly on her judgment of what other people think of her. This may not be what these other people *actually* think of her, but what she *thinks* they think of her. The tragedy lies in the fact that most of us so seldom verbalize how much we like each other that we all go through life basing our opinions of ourselves on impressions gleaned from nonverbal communication.

All of us want our children to have a healthy amount of self-esteem. Because of this, it is important to analyze exactly what we are communicating to them, because if they have to guess how we feel about them, they may guess wrong. The other day our daughter came back to the house at ten minutes after eight and said she had missed the bus. She kept a tactful silence while I got ready to drive her to school, but as we went out the door, she asked, "Are you mad at me?" That was a perfectly logical conclusion to draw from my demeanor, but in fact I was disgusted with the bus driver because he had left the corner before the scheduled time. It was not my daughter's fault, and I made sure she understood that as quickly as possible.

We are told that children blame themselves for everything from divorce to the death of a loved one. They realize that their very existence causes people a lot of work and expense (we usually make sure they know just how much!), and they tend to feel that everything would go along more smoothly if they weren't around. Parents need to reassure children that they are not the cause of every family hardship and instead let them know that life would be very empty without them.

One of my particular peeves is the way some people seem to need to know whether or not every child was "planned." Why anyone is interested in such information is beyond me. I can't imagine what effect it has on a child to hear that he was unplanned, or to be called "our little mistake" or "an accident," or to have a parent say, "We were hoping for a girl." Christians can always say their child was planned, if someone should have the poor taste to inquire. God planned their child's life.

We should be careful what we say about our children in their presence, for they will remember it. I have personally had people refer to their child as "our little devil," or say, "I can't do anything with her," with the child standing right there! Each statement our child hears us make about him becomes a part of his self-image, along with all the verbal and nonverbal impressions he receives from us and other important people in his life. We must guard our tongues, because we cannot unsay words spoken out of carelessness or in anger; and our children accept our evaluation of them as being true.

The burden for parents, then, is that their child's self-esteem depends on them. If they esteem the child highly, the child will place a high value on himself. Before he ever goes to school or clashes with friends or takes his lumps in the outside world, he has already received the basic idea of how much he is worth from his parents.

How, then, can parents communicate to their children the high value they place upon them? How can they build self-esteem in their children?

Acceptance

First of all, they must accept their children *as they are.* Parents who try to turn a noncompetitive child into an athlete, or a mechanically minded child into a scholar, are not accepting the child they have and are damaging his self-esteem. "They would like me if I were an athlete or scholar," the child reasons, "but since I am neither of those things, I must not be worth much to them."

Accepting children as they are can be a problem for every parent but is even more difficult for parents of handicapped children. The desire for our children to be healthy, fit, and perfect is hard to overcome; but we must set aside these desires and fall in instead with God's plan for the child who has a disability. We must respond to God's call to look beyond the surface traits and treasure the handicapped child for the abilities and personality he has, not destroy his sense of self-worth because of our inability to accept the absence of the attributes he does not have.

I am continually amazed at the resistance most parents show to any suggestion that their child might have even a slight disability. I remember the time a new neighbor and I were talking, when her daughter, about six or seven years of age, walked right out into the street in front of a car. It was obvious to me that the child had not heard the car coming, but the mother spanked her soundly and flared up in anger at me when I asked if the girl had ever had her hearing checked. "There's nothing wrong with her hearing!" she yelled. Apparently it was more acceptable to the woman that her daughter be so careless as to endanger her life than that she might be hard of hearing.

As a teacher, I often had a difficult time getting parents to admit that some behavior of their child was not normal and should be checked. A child has a right to feel, "My parents won't face up to this problem I really have, so they don't like the real me; they like the fake me they have built up in their minds." Thus his sense of self-worth decreases.

No one is perfect. This simple fact seems to escape the reason of some parents. If we hope for perfect children we will be disappointed, and our disappointment will harm our children's view of themselves. Everyone has eye trouble, back trouble, or skin trouble, or needs braces or some kind of operation, or can't do something well no matter how hard they try. We must all accept each other for what we *are,* rather than worrying about what we are not. This is important for all of us, and especially for our vulnerable children.

Not Pushing

We also build self-esteem in our children when we allow them to advance at their own pace *and do not hurry them* into situations and activities beyond their level of maturity. When their children are little, mothers can hardly wait until the youngsters are old enough to do things for themselves. They especially tend to push the oldest child into the next stage of development as fast as possible. Afterwards, they may realize too late how soon the baby stage is over and how special the feeling of the child's dependence and closeness really was. They may begin to enjoy each phase with younger children instead of fighting it . . . and then wonder why the older child is jealous of the younger! Children who are not forced to grow up faster than they should have a better self-image.

Discipline

Disciplined children feel better about themselves than undisciplined children. Children who know how to behave correctly receive approval from friends, parents, teachers, and even strangers; and gaining the approval of others is one of man's basic needs. Equally important is the inner sense of pride and well-being that comes from knowing you have done the right thing, even if no one is around to pat you on the back. Parents who do not teach their children how to act in a manner that gains the approval of society make it much more difficult for them to develop a good self-image. A child who sees people cringe when he comes into view cannot feel very good about himself.

Self-esteem can either be enhanced or damaged by the *way in which parents administer discipline.* Someone has coined the phrase, "Break a child's will but not his spirit"; and parents should remember that it is possible to discipline in a way that wounds a child deeply. Proverbs 18:14 says, "The spirit of a man can endure his sickness, but a broken spirit who can bear?" (NASB). And Proverbs 17:22 echoes, ". . . a broken spirit dries up the bones" (NASB).

If we want to be sure our correction does not damage our child's self-esteem, we should remember the following:

1. Use "preventive discipline" often so the amount of "corrective discipline" can be reduced. Praise, praise, praise! Make your children aware of the many things they do well, and they will be able to take their mistakes and lack of abilities in stride. Control their environment without smothering them, and issue needed warnings to help them stay out of trouble. Reward their good behavior with your attention and in other ways.

2. Decide on the behavior that is important to you and insist on it, but do not pick away at a child over minor matters. Overcoerced children are nervous and often have a low opinion of themselves. Some mothers have a rule about *everything,* especially with their first child. They seem to feel there is only one right way to put a book on a shelf, or pick up leaves, or even play with a toy. If it really makes a difference, for example, which outfit your child puts on, don't hesitate to say so. Otherwise, let him choose, and enhance his confidence in himself by complimenting him on his choice.

3. Reject wrong behavior without rejecting the child. Sometimes we act as though a wrong deed has made the person entirely evil. We use phrases such as "You *always* . . . ," or "You *never.* . . ." Our message should not be, "I don't like *you,*" but "I don't like what you *did.*"

Mr. Rogers, of the children's television show, sings a song that parents would do well to remember. The lyrics go something like this: "Good people do bad things sometimes, some of the time they do. Don't you? The very same people who are good sometimes are the very same people who are bad sometimes. Funny, but it's true. It's the same for me, isn't it the same for you?"[1]

4. Discipline in private whenever possible. Adults do not like to be censured in front of their colleagues at work, but often seem to forget that embarrassment matters to their children. If possible, even brothers and sisters should be excluded from the scene. Sometimes siblings enjoy seeing each other in trouble; this should not be encouraged. Protecting a child's self-esteem means showing consideration for his feelings when administering discipline, especially spanking. However, a child who challenges your authority in public had better be prepared to accept the consequences in public.

Another reason to discipline in private is so that the parent will not be tempted to try to get other children to side in with them against the child who is being disciplined. Adult authority is plenty for a child to face without having the burden also of the disapproval of friends or siblings.

5. Be consistent. If you let some behavior go unmentioned one time and then jump all over the child another time, you embarrass and confuse him and wound his spirit. If your discipline depends on your mood or the activity you happen to be involved in, you are not being consistent. If you let the opinions of adults who may be present shape your discipline, if you "play to your audience," being more or less lenient in order to win their approval, you are being unfair to your child. You are using him to build yourself up in someone else's eyes, and he will know it, and his sense of self-worth will be diminished. Your standards should be the same whether you are on the telephone, in a store, or at home, whether you are alone, or with your mother-in-law, or with your pastor.

6. Be fair. This is even more difficult than being consistent. Being fair does not mean you give Child A as many spankings

or privileges as Child B; he may not deserve them. It does mean you have the same standard of conduct for a boy as for a girl. It does not mean that you give children identical gifts, because an item rarely has the same value for two different people, and a gift should be chosen with the individual in mind. It may mean that you keep a written record showing at what age you advanced allowances, bedtimes, etc., so you at least know what you did, whether you choose to give each succeeding child those privileges or not.

A parent can expect that some children will often question the fairness of a decision and so should weigh opinions carefully before the final judgment is made. But children can accept almost any decision on the part of an adult *if they are convinced that the adult is striving to be fair.* This confidence is *earned* on the basis of past performance.

A person's sense of self-worth increases when they know that other people take their feelings seriously, when it is important to someone that they be treated fairly. When a child is treated unfairly and no one cares, their self-image is damaged.

A mother who desires to act in a godly manner must also be careful *not to be partial to one child over another,* "For God does not show favoritism" (Rom. 2:11). James also warns against personal favoritism and states, "But if you show favoritism, you sin . . ." (James 2:1, 9).

Just as in the church it is possible to greet the rich or attractive people warmly and let less-pleasing people fend for themselves, so we may treat a child who seems to us to be more winsome with more consideration. The reverse may also be true. Sometimes a troublesome or handicapped child will have the entire family life geared to meeting his needs and will receive all the attention, while less-demanding siblings are ignored.

Mothers must take care that they do not always decide in favor of the more verbal child, the one who presents the arguments on his side the most persuasively, or assume that a difficult child is always wrong. When parents show favoritism, the spirit of the wronged child is damaged, and the character of the child who receives better than he deserves is not developed properly. But when children know their parents strive to be impartial, all relationships within the family flourish.

7. Be reasonable. Do not use a cannon to kill a gnat. The punishment must fit the crime; and before sentencing there must be some opportunity to explain any extenuating circumstances. Those who act first and ask questions later are rarely either reasonable or fair.

Use tactics appropriate to the age group. For young children, punishment that lasts for days can be unbearable, since a week to them seems as long as a month to an adult. Even for older children we should realize that discipline that extends over a long period of time also extends the pain and humiliation over the same amount of time and may cause a certain amount of alienation from parents for the duration as well. Such tactics should be reserved for the most serious situations or repeated offenses.

When God said, "Come now, let us reason together," He at least meant that communication was allowed and He was approachable (Isa. 1:18). Mothers should always be ready both to listen to and to explain fully the conflicting points of view involved in any situation. Reasonable people rarely leave a trail of wounded egos in their wake.

8. Apologize for mistakes in discipline. Mothers are not always right. We know this but sometimes neglect to admit it to our children, fearing it will lessen our authority in the home.

Children respond positively to honest people. If we have been unreasonable or unfair, if we have overreacted or not taken one of their hurts seriously enough, we should take steps to rectify the mistake. We will not always be able to nullify the results of our incorrect action—you cannot unscramble eggs—but we can restore our relationship with the injured party.

One of the greatest problems in marriage and other human relationships is the inability of people to ask for forgiveness. If we teach our children how to confess their sins by doing it to them, if we tell them we are sorry for mistreating them, we not only heal the immediate problem, we increase their ability to express the same feelings to us and to others.

Jesus said that if our brother has something against us, we should leave our offering at the altar and go and get it straightened out before continuing our worship (Matt. 5:23-24). Mothers cannot continue in a "business as usual" manner and ignore their responsibility to be reconciled to their children. "Our brother" may be our child.

The way we discipline, then, can either help build or tear down a child's self-esteem. A child who feels rejected when corrected will be hurt; but a child who knows that his parents will take the time to be fair, consistent, and reasonable will feel important and will survive correction with his sense of worth intact.

Sibling Relationships

Another area of family life that is crucial to a child's self-image is that of *sibling relationships*. Children gain or lose self-esteem depending on how these relationships progress. A strong, caring family circle which includes every member will produce more self-esteem. If any one of the members is not involved in this caring relationship, all lose something important.

There is no reason to expect that children will just naturally adore one another simply because they happen to be born into the same family. For that reason it is dangerous to allow their relationships to develop without any attention from the parents.

Mothers should expect neither too much nor too little from the relationships between brothers and sisters. Without making a big deal out of it, parents should not expect a child to be thrilled at having to share everything (parental attention, space, food, the TV) with another child. They should keep in mind that no human beings get along perfectly all the time, and that people who live in such close quarters as a family have even more reason to become irritated with each other. They should be aware that grandparents, friends, or teachers may show favoritism toward one child over another and that there are many other sources of friction.

On the other hand, while being honest about the problems involved, parents can help greatly by stressing the advantages of having brothers and sisters. Companionship, strength, and increased love are possible in a larger family. Psalm 127:5 suggests the safety in numbers that children and parents can feel. Children can grow to appreciate each other as they realize that no one on this earth will ever know and understand them like their own brother or sister does. No wife or husband will remember childhood incidents with them; no friend will understand the points of view that held sway in their home and influenced them as children. No matter how close they become to other people in life, only the members of their family do not need to have the basic things about their lives and background explained to them.

When they move to another city, all relationships must start at the beginning again except for those within the family. When a pet or family member dies, only those in the family share their loss. So when a mother sees one child being abusive to another, she can take him aside and say with conviction, "I'd be a little more careful about how you treat him if I were you. He is an important person in your life and will very likely be the best friend you will ever have."

Family loyalty, good feelings toward one's brothers and

sisters, pride in the accomplishments of family members—all these enhance self-esteem. That is, the skills and attainments of family members add to the self-esteem of all *if* the accomplishments of one are not used as weapons against others. If you use the A's on Tommy's report card as an opportunity to take a dig at Jimmy, you will both make Jimmy resent Tommy and take the joy out of the A's for Tommy, all in one stroke.

Never use the accomplishments of one child as a "lesson" for another. You destroy their feelings of pride in each other, their loyalty, and you attack their self-esteem by acting as if all your children should be equally good at everthing, which is, of course, impossible. If Jimmy's grades need attention, that should be dealt with in private and *with no reference whatsoever* to Tommy's report card. Jimmy should not get good grades because Tommy did; we should all do our best in everything because that is the right thing to do. We never do anything because someone else does it, do we? We do something because it is either right or wrong in itself.

If a child's room is dirty, you say, "Go clean your room." You do not say, "Why can't you keep your room clean like Mary does?" You never say, "Why can't you be thoughtful like . . . ?" or suggest that they do *anything* like another person. If a thing is right, it should be done for its own sake, without any reference to another human being.

One child's successes should never reflect in any way but a good way on another member of the family. Otherwise, self-esteem is damaged. Each person should be prized for what he is. Children are not in a contest for their parents' love in a healthy family.

Explaining Life Situations

Mothers can also help their children to feel good about themselves by *helping them to make sense out of life,* to understand the tangled human relationships surrounding them, to grasp the meaning of daily events. Young people are quick to pick up emotional undercur,ents. They see the stress in people's faces and hear the strain in their voices more readily than adults. They often mull over the scenes they have observed and come to wrong conclusions. They also often ask questions about events months after they happen, and mothers need to have their wits about them in order to properly cope with the delayed reaction children often have to things they have seen and heard.

This morning my daughter was eating breakfast and I was packing her lunch for school. "Why did Mr. So-and-so cry?" she asked. She was referring to an incident that had taken place eight months before and which she had never mentioned.

I thought a minute. "Well, he had just heard that someone died."

"Oh," she replied. But I could tell she was not satisfied, and she was right not to be. Another element, which she had evidently perceived, was involved in the situation, but I did not know how to explain it. "Who died?" she asked.

I told her the man's name.

Finally I said, "The reason Mr. So-and-so was so upset was that he had been angry with the man who died, but he died before they could get the problem straightened out."

"Oh!" she replied, with more satisfaction. After a few seconds, she said, "I didn't know daddies cried . . . or mommies . . . at least very often."

"Well," I answered, "they don't cry over every cut finger." And we both laughed.

Adults are correctly hesitant to tell children private information about other people's lives. Children have a unique gift of blabbing things in their piercing little voices at the worst possible moment. However, if Aunt Minnie has a drinking problem that makes her behavior erratic, your child is affected. If Uncle Oliver spouts racial slurs at family gatherings, your children hear them, too. A child is involved in hundreds of situations which confuse him and leave him feeling that he is powerless to understand and cope with life.

Knowledge is power. When a child knows what is really going on around him, he feels more "grown up," and his faith in his ability to meet the challenges of life increases. Parents owe it to their children to tell them the truth about any situation if the child is old enough to handle the truth and if the parents can honorably do so. Their explanations should include proper cautions about repeating private matters of other people.

The Book of Proverbs has a great deal to say about wisdom. Often this refers to spiritual wisdom, but wisdom in human relationships is also emphasized. In Proverbs, the father is often speaking to the son, urging him to become wise. "My son, pay attention to my wisdom, listen well to my words of insight, that you may maintain discretion and your lips may preserve knowledge" (5:1-2). "Listen, my sons, to a father's instruction, pay attention and gain understanding. . . . Wisdom is supreme; therefore get wisdom. Though it cost you all you have, get understanding" (4:1, 7).

How is a child going to gain wisdom unless his parents instruct him? How is he going to understand why we can talk about babies in one place but not another unless someone explains that Mrs. So-and-so just had her third miscarriage? How can children learn to show consideration for people's feelings if they don't know what those are? When they are let in on some of the mysteries of life, they can begin to read people's reactions more correctly by themselves and can become sensitive, caring individuals on their own. The knowledge and wisdom and understanding they have developed give them confidence as they face life, confidence that they can cope successfully with the varied kinds of situations our confused world presents.

The Bible says, "Therefore encourage one another and build each other up" (1 Thess. 5:11). This is the task of the mother who wants to increase her child's self-esteem. In order to know how best to build up each of her children, she must *get to know them individually.* This is not the same as loving them and more than simply having their best interests at heart. It means that she must spend enough time with each one to know what he likes or doesn't like, what he thinks is funny or important, what joys and sorrows he is experiencing in life, what he dreams about or hopes for.

It means that she is involved more often in pleasant activities with him—reading, talking, crafts, cooking, walks, sports—than in disciplining him, and that at least some of these are done with him apart from other children. A child's self-image is not enhanced much if the only attention he gets is when he's in trouble.

You would think that people made in the image of God would have no self-image problems at all. That, of course, was God's intention. But sin entered, and ever since, our relationships with a fallen creation and other fallen people have damaged our good feelings about ourselves. In Christ, however, our self-image is restored (Rom. 8:29) and our worth established (5:8). We and our children are to see ourselves as being so valuable to God that He would die for us, as in fact He did.

Mothers must do their best to protect their children from the onslaughts of the world that will try to undermine their sense of worth, as well as steer a proper course in the home. To know exactly how to meet the needs of the differing personalities who are her children is not easy, but it is her task.

"And we urge you, brethren, admonish the unruly, encourage the fainthearted, help the weak, be patient with all" (1 Thess. 5:14 NASB).

Making It Personal

1. Upon what is a person's sense of self-esteem based?

_____

_____

_____

2. Why is it important to express verbally the things we like about one another? _____

_____

_____

_____

3. Why must parents be extremely careful about the comments they make to and about their children? _____

_____

_____

_____

4. Can you recall from your own childhood your time of greatest anxiety? embarrassment? disappointment? joy? What attitude toward our children should these memories encourage? (See Col. 3:12; Luke 15:20; Rom. 12:15.) _____

_____

_____

_____

5. List as many things that affect self-esteem as you can find in the chapter. _____

_____

_____

_____

6. If we are created in the image of God, why do we have so much trouble with self-esteem? _____

_____

_____

_____

7. How can these Scriptures help increase a person's feelings of self-worth: Genesis 1:27, 31; Psalm 8:4–6; John 3:16; Romans 8:15–17? _____

_____

_____

8. How does Ecclesiastes 4:9-12 apply to sibling relationships? _____

_____

_____

9. How would the following affect children's attitudes toward other children in the family:
   a. Mother holds baby as she says in a teasing voice to her two-year-old, "Johnny, look what Mommy has." _____

_____

   b. Mother spanks an eight-year-old child because he did not keep his four-year-old sibling out of the mud. _____

_____

   c. Parents insist their high-schooler take an eleven-year-old sibling to the school's football games. _____

_____

10. Why is it harmful to compare one person to another (Rom. 12:4–8)? _____

_____

Before you read on. . . . Do you attempt to guide your children in their dealings with each other? / How do you feel about "tattling"? / How do you handle problems that arise between you and an adult neighbor? / How are squabbles between your children and neighbor children dealt with? / What is God's standard for human relationships? Read John 13:34-35. / Would you say that most adults handle disagreements well?

13

GETTING ALONG TOGETHER

Two women were talking when the son and daughter of one of them, furious with each other, interrupted their conversation. Accusations flew back and forth until the mother said calmly, "Go settle it yourselves." The children protested loudly, both wanting justice. "Go settle it yourselves," she repeated. Each gave the other a shove and started shouting recriminations at each other. "Go away. I don't want to hear about it," the mother said. The boy went storming off; the girl went the other direction with tears in her eyes. The mother smiled, shook her head, and went on talking to her friend.

This is a scene familiar to all of us. Did the mother react correctly? How are we supposed to handle the daily squabbles which arise in every home?

First of all, let us examine various courses of action available to us when disputes arise.

1. Discussion and agreement.
2. Discussion without solution—agree to disagree.
3. Argument in which one person "out-talks" another, overpowering another with verbal skill although he might be in the wrong.
4. Verbal abuse, with the more vitriolic emerging as victor.
5. Threat of physical or emotional harm (spoken or unspoken).
6. Cold silence.
7. Walking away, leaving the other person alone.
8. Physical force.

When we consider the alternatives, we come to realize that while we may at times decide to "let the kids work things out themselves," as parents we should always be aware of just how things *are* working out.

If we have goals regarding the relationships between our children, if we hope they will be loving and loyal to each other, we must realize that children do not naturally have either the knowledge nor the expertise to handle many of the problems that inevitably arise when people live together. Many adults do not have the ability to solve interpersonal problems, either, and go through life handicapped. They tend to gripe about situations or become embroiled in extended feuds rather than resolve problems with positive courses of action.

The Bible, so practical in every way, gives us a great deal of help in this area of life as well. First of all, it portrays graphically for us the fact that people are different. The disciples did not see everything eye to eye. The twelve sons of Jacob displayed great individuality. There was much diversity among the men and women God chose and used for His purposes.

Men and women also differ in their approach to life. All efforts to make us unisexual to the contrary, a real divergence exists between the male and the female mind set, and this crops up in our adolescent boys and girls as well.

Our origins and backgrounds, our attitudes and personalities, our maleness or femaleness, even our spiritual gifts affect us so that even as Christians we do not view everything from the same angle. Our discussion of character and personality traits in chapter 10 emphasized the many acceptable differences that can be found in any group of people, including those who live together.

Despite all this, the Bible clearly teaches that God has made it possible for us to get along with each other and even to love and enjoy one another. The Book of Proverbs and the letters of Paul are particularly filled with instructions about how to live together as Christians and as families: "Do not think of yourself more highly than you ought, but . . . with sober judgment" (Rom. 12:3). "Consider others better than [yourself]" (Phil. 2:3). "Submit to one another" (Eph. 5:21). "Speak . . . the truth in love" (4:15). "Live peaceable and quiet lives" (1 Tim. 2:2). "Look not only to your own interests, but also to the interests of others" (Phil. 2:4).

But in Matthew 18 we have the clearest teaching of the exact steps to take in settling disputes. The intention of the passage is primarily to give direction regarding church discipline: how to deal with straying sheep (v. 12), members of a church who are involved in some sinful act. However, these principles should also apply to the family, which is the church in the home.

Let us see how the steps of Matthew 18 would work in the family. Verses 15 and 16 say, "If your brother sins against you, go and show him his fault, just between the two of you. If he listens to you, you have won your brother over. But if he will not listen, take one or two others along, so that 'every matter may be established by the testimony of two or three witnesses.'"

When Sally comes to you with a complaint about Johnny, you respond, "Have you talked to Johnny about it?" If not, you advise her to do so. At this point she may decide just to let the matter drop, that it is not worth all the hassle. This is where inveterate talebearers will quit. But the problem is that the Bible does not say, "If your brother sins against you, let it slide." If the complaint is a silly one, I would not push for any further action. If, however, it is something that should be settled in order not to harm the children's relationship or in order to build their characters, Sally should be encouraged to go to Johnny and discuss it.

When Sally approaches Johnny, she should try to avoid inflammatory words and accusing tones and simply state the situation as she sees it and express her feelings about it. A very young child, for example, might say, "I don't like it when you push me. It hurts." If Johnny does not respond in a satisfactory way, then Sally may come to the mother, who becomes the "witness" referred to in verse 16.

Many mothers refuse to become involved in settling disputes between their children, discharging their parental responsibility with a curt, "Don't be a tattletale!" This kind of response does not fulfill either the scriptural role of witness nor the injunction to bear one another's burdens. What it does do is reject the child and perhaps further victimize the already injured party in the dispute by calling him a tattletale. I have seen both parents and teachers turn away children with legitimate, serious grievances with just such name-calling tactics. Such laziness can hardly be loving; such judgment can hardly be fair.

Often the substance of the complaint does not seem that important to adults, but children have an exquisite sensitivity to right and wrong, a trait that Christian parents want to encourage. We want morality to matter to our children, so we must deal with it on their level.

What we hope for, of course, is that the whole process will end at step one, "If he listens to you, you have won your brother over." We want children to learn not to come to the witness until they have approached the offender privately. Children will feel better toward one another if they know that none of them will go to the parents with an accusation until they have discussed the matter with the other person involved, and that even after that they will not complain to anyone but the witness. Our churches would be greatly helped if their members learned these steps for handling problems as children.

Another biblical model mothers might employ in settling their children's disputes is that of the judge, which we find in the Old Testament from Moses to Solomon. The Israelites brought their litigation to a leader and abided by his decision. Even if the children use the principles outlined in Matthew 18, the mother will often end up in the role of judge, deciding who was in the wrong and meting justice where required.

Any mother who wants her children to learn the importance of doing right and being fair must be diligent about such things in her own home. She must not side-step her opportunities to teach these values but should remember the scriptural injunctions, "Speak up and judge fairly; defend the rights of the poor and needy" (Prov. 31:9) and, "Stop judging by mere appearances, and make a right judgment" (John 7:24).

Of the eight possible responses to disagreements listed at the beginning of the chapter, only two or three are appropriate for Christians, whether adults or children. Proverbs 15:1 reminds us that "a harsh word stirs up anger." Arguing results in the frustration of the less verbal person rather than achieving a just solution. Verbal abuse, threats, or physical force are not Christian options. Silence is not a satisfactory way of dealing with problems, and, like walking away, should be permitted only in order to get oneself in hand until one is able to face the situation more calmly. After all, it is a "gentle answer" which "turns away wrath," not stoney silence or a stiff-legged retreat.

The best way our children will learn how to respond to life's misunderstandings, of course, is to see us modeling this kind of behavior with our husbands, neighbors, mothers-in-law, and within the church family. If we remain angry and grow bitter because we will not go to a person and discuss with them the way they offended us, our children will probably copy our actions rather than follow scriptural principles.

The law of the jungle, the survival of the fittest, is not the law of Christian love. After all, the fittest in spiritual things and in God's eyes are not those who emerge victorious from bloody, vicious encounters. Christ said, "Blessed are the poor in spirit, . . . Blessed are the meek, . . . Blessed are the pure in heart, . . . Blessed are the peacemakers" (Matt. 5:3, 5, 8-9).

Family relationships are of utmost importance to God and to the developing characters and personalities of our children. Our goal as mothers is to help our children keep their hearts and consciences pure (1 Tim. 1:5). One of the ways we can accomplish this is by helping them to maintain healthy relationships with brothers, sisters, parents, and friends—relationships untainted by guilt, bitterness, power struggles, or regret.

Making It Personal

1. What are eight ways human beings handle disputes?

_____

_____

_____

2. Which of these are options for Christians? _____

_____

_____

_____

3. What kind of relationship between our children do we want to encourage? _____

_____

_____

4. How can the steps in Matthew 18 be applied to family disputes? _____

_____

_____

_____

5. How active should a mother be in settling problems between children? _____

_____

_____

_____

_____

6. How prepared are your children to settle disputes among themselves? _____

_____

_____

_____

_____

7. What action on the part of parents caused problems between children in Genesis 25:27-28 and 37:3-11? _____

_____

_____

8. From what did some of the bad feelings between Jacob's sons stem? (Compare Gen. 35:22-26 with 37:3 and 42:36-38.) How could this be applied to the step-family situation today? _____

_____

_____

_____

9. How do you handle disagreements with your husband? What are your children learning from watching you? _____

_____

_____

Before you read on. . . . What do you think parents owe their children? / Do you feel your parents deprived you of any basic right? If so, what? / Are you denying your children anything that is rightfully theirs? / What effect does an irritable parent have on a child? Read Proverbs 21:9, 19. / What are some sources of family tension? Read Proverbs 22:24-25; 2 Corinthians 6:14. / Why is it important for parents to correct any areas of sin in their lives? See Matthew 18:6.

14

A CHILD'S BILL OF RIGHTS

In England and in the United States there existed for many decades a general understanding of the liberties and privileges due the citizens of those nations. Nevertheless, in each country a time came when the people demanded that their rights be set down in a permanent form so that they could never be denied.

In the non-too-distant past, there was also a general consensus regarding the family—what constituted a family, what was expected of it, its place in society. We had not identified intact families, nuclear families, one-parent families, or extended families. People generally agreed about how children should be reared, what values were important, and what kind of life they hoped to provide for their offspring. Unfortunately, this is no longer true. Age-old values are being questioned on every side, the family itself is dismissed by some as nonessential, and the claims of children upon their parents are obscured in a tangle of contradictory opinions.

But the light of God's sure Word sends its penetrating beam through the confusion and disorder of man's ideas, its clear message reminding us that He knows how things ought to be, that He is the One who created families in the first place and His plan is the right one. In the Bible God has made plain the requirements of the godly life, including His ideas about godly parenthood. Man may be unsure about what he owes to his children, but God is not. He has set down some obligations which parents hold toward their children, outlined in Scripture in permanent form as a sort of Bill of Rights, basic needs children are entitled to have met by their parents.

Secure Relationships

A child has the right to have a mother and father who remain married to each other and who love and respect each other.

A few years ago this statement would have needed no documentation. People agreed that God's plan was for parents to love each other and stay married until one of them died. Now, however, with homes breaking up on every side, people are expressing the opinion that divorce is really the best solution much of the time, that it is not as harmful as it used to be. This is not God's view.

God's ideas about the family have not changed. In Ephesians 5:22–6:4, the Bible states clearly the kind of family relationship God intends. The father is to love his wife and children; the mother is to respect and be submissive to her husband; and the children are to obey their parents. God is the same yesterday, today, and forever (Heb. 13:8); and Jesus' primary answer to questions about divorce was, "What God has joined together, let man not separate" (Matt. 19:6; Mark 10:9).

The common statement of the day, however, is that the parents must "do what is right for them"—a phrase, ironically enough, which has become synonymous with getting a divorce. Young people, we are told, are more sophisticated now. They understand that "these things happen." It is increasingly obvious to all of us that "these things happen," but what children are not prepared for is its happening to *them.*

Divorce not only shatters a child's secure world, it deprives him or her of the direct attention and interest of one parent. No matter how much the father may love the child, if he is living elsewhere, estrangement increases; if the father's relationship with the child was already weak, separation often severs it entirely. The diagram below shows the situation caused by most divorces.

Remarriage, however, which increasingly enters the picture, jeopardizes and often destroys the relationship not only with the distant parent, but between the child and the parent with whom he lives. We tend to forget that people who plan to remarry usually date a series of individuals beforehand. Dating not only takes up a great deal of their quality free time but also brings a succession of dating partners into the lives of the children as well. If the mother and father both remarry, their relationships could be charted in this manner:

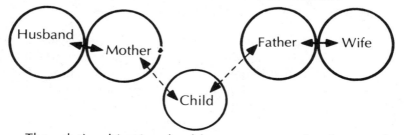

The relationships involved become tremendously complicated, since each child and adult will respond to each other person in the situation differently. But no matter how the parents view things, most children at this point feel they no longer claim the primary interest of either mother or father. In essence, they have lost their rightful place in the lives of both parents.

After remarriage, each parent is anxious to "make this one work"; and in the first thrilling months of love, children feel even more left out than ever. If the children live with their mother, they must adjust to a new head of the house. He does things differently: he has irritating habits, wants meals to conform to his tastes and schedule, and enjoys spending his leisure time in ways foreign to the youngsters' experience.

Occasionally, this may be viewed by the children as a change for the better. More often, though they do not always verbalize it, they feel involved in mortal combat with the new member of the family, with the prize being the mother's love and attention and the sort of family life they were used to. For the father, his remarriage often so dilutes the amount of effort he is willing to invest in keeping in contact with his children as to virtually estrange him from them.

Many of the same problems also arise in the event of the death of a parent and the survivor's remarriage. However, even though a child sometimes feels angry at the deceased parent for dying and leaving him in a more difficult state, at least he can reassure himself that (except for suicide) the parent couldn't help it. He has no such comfort in divorce.

With divorce, at least one of his parents, and sometimes both, show that they are unwilling to do whatever is necessary to sustain the family. A child tends to take this personally. "If I were lovable enough," he reasons, "if I were worth enough, nothing on earth could force my parent to separate from me."

Someone can say to him, "This isn't your problem. It has nothing to do with you." But the child knows it *is* his problem, one that will affect him for the rest of his life. When two trains collide, it is not "the engineer's problem" to the passengers. If a surgeon's scalpel slips, it is not "the doctor's problem" to the patient.

Fathers as well as mothers must realize that they cannot shrug off the possibility of permanent damage to the spirits of their children which may result from any decision to separate or divorce. Malachi 2:15-16 warns of spiritual jeopardy in which divorce places children: "And what does he desire? Godly offspring. So take heed to yourselves, and let none be faithless to the wife of his youth. For I hate divorce, says the LORD the God of Israel" (RSV).

Many marriages, even Christian marriages, fall far short of the loving relationship God intended. Staying together for the good of the children is not enough, just as sullen obedience does not fulfill the Lord's expectations of a child's attitude toward his parents. Often people who are willing to spend all kinds of time improving their bridge or golf game, or to pray for years for someone's salvation, will not put the same work, prayer, and faith effort into a faltering marriage.

God is still working miracles today, and I have personally witnessed many marriages saved by the grace of God. Often it is the wife who first has to humble herself and make changes that will bring her attitudes into conformity with God's will, loving and respecting her husband for months or even years before he begins to respond.

However, to do any less—to live in constant tension or to let the relationship deteriorate to the point of separation or divorce—is to deny our children one of their God-ordained rights. The risk of harming our children is not one that can be taken lightly. As Jesus said, "But if anyone causes one of these little ones who believe in me to sin, it would be better for him to have a large millstone hung around his neck and to be drowned in the depths of the sea. Woe to the world because of the things that cause people to sin. Such things must come, but woe to the man through whom they come!" (Matt. 18:6-7).

Parental Love

A child has the right to be loved by his parents.

Since parents are erring, self-centered human beings, we need to be reminded that God has called us to look beyond ourselves and love our children. The kind of love God wants us to express is not weak or sentimental, but durable and full of healthy emotion.

God has set the example for love of father to child: "How great is the love the Father has lavished on us, that we should be called children of God!" (1 John 3:1). "As a father has compassion on his children, so the LORD has compassion on those who fear him" (Ps. 103:13).

God has also established the form of mother-child love: "You shall be nursed, you shall be carried on the hip and fondled on the knees. As one whom his mother comforts, so I will comfort you" (Isa. 66:12-13 NASB). The Bible's primary command for mothers is that they love their children (Titus 2:4).

It is easy to lose sight of our children's inner needs and become caught up in the mechanics of daily living and the pressures of outside activities. We can view our children as a means of enhancing our image and become preoccupied with how their actions reflect on us. While it is natural to care about how we appear to others, our first responsibility is to express loving concern toward our children.

Our children did not ask us to bring them into the world. Since we did, they have a right to our love. "My command is this: Love each other as I have loved you" (John 15:12).

Parental Provision

A child has a right to be provided for by his parents.

This right of children is generally accepted, but we can see the wisdom of God in making the duty of parents to support their children a permanent part of Scripture. For there is a disturbing anti-child spirit in some circles today where children are considered by parents as a drain on the family resources and impediments in the path of their own self-fulfillment. But the Bible sets the record straight when it says, "Children should not have to save up for their parents, but parents for their children" (2 Cor. 12:14).

Fathers are specifically warned not to evade their responsibility as breadwinners, for 1 Timothy 5:8 states, "If anyone does not provide for his relatives, and especially for his immediate family, he has denied the faith and is worse than an unbeliever."

Mothers also are encouraged in Scripture to take good care

of their children. The "excellent wife" in Proverbs 31 rises early to give food to her family and looks well to the ways of her household; she clothes her children, not in the cheapest fabric she can find, but in scarlet.

As in all things, God has shown us how we ought to provide for our children, since he "richly provides us with everything for our enjoyment" (1 Tim. 6:17). God, in His love, gives to His children. Our joy will come in following His pattern, for we will then be providing for our children in accordance with His will.

Discipline and Instruction

A child has the right to be reared in the discipline and instruction of the Lord.

Parents tend to think of the religious instruction of their children as *their duty* rather than their *children's right;* but Ephesians 6:4 can be interpreted to mean that if we withhold discipline and instruction, we may provoke our children to anger by so doing. Parents who are lax in teaching scriptural principles to their offspring are denying them their very ability to know God and become pleasing to Him. Jesus said people fall into error because they do not know the Scriptures or the power of God (Mark 12:24), and children must depend on their parents to teach them.

Family devotions—studying the Bible and praying together —not only are an important part of a child's spiritual growth, but are a means of binding the family together on a spiritual plane. Mother, father, and children may all go their separate ways during the day, but family devotions remind them of their common goal and oneness in Christ. Every Christian bookstore is filled with materials suitable for use with children of all ages.

But study and prayer together in the home only rounds out a total plan for nurturing, which includes faithful church attendance and continuous teaching and spiritual guidance in life situations (Deut. 11:19-21).

Parents must be sure that both their instruction and their discipline is "of the Lord." God's standards and God's methods must be used. The vast majority of children across this land are being denied their right to a godly upbringing, and both they and our country will suffer because of it.

These, then, are the rights specifically given to children by Scripture. Parents who love each other and their children, who provide for their children, and who teach them God's ways are fulfilling His will for their families. May the Lord continue to help us all keep these simple commands faithfully.

Making It Personal

1. What does God say about the marriage bond? Read 1 Corinthians 7:10-11; Malachi 2:13-16; Romans 7:2-3.

_____

_____

_____

2. Read Ephesians 5:22–6:4 and discuss the roles of family members approved by God. _____

_____

_____

_____

3. What is the first right of children mentioned in this chapter? _____

_____

_____

_____

4. How does divorce of parents affect children? (Include a study of Mal. 2:15-16 in different versions.) _____

_____

_____

_____

_____

5. How does death of a parent affect children? _____

_____

_____

_____

_____

6. How does remarriage of divorced parents affect children?

_____

_____

_____

_____

7. How does remarriage of a widowed parent affect children?

_____

_____

_____

_____

8. Discuss the other three rights of children. _____

_____

_____

_____

9. What should be included in the "discipline and instruction of the Lord"? _____

_____

_____

_____

_____

10. Read aloud, "A Mother's Prayer" on the next page. Does this prayer contain your goals as a mother? _____

_____

_____

_____

_____

11. Identify and commit specfic areas of need to the Lord in prayer. _____

_____

_____

_____

_____

A Mother's Prayer

The Bible records a beautiful prayer in John 17, the prayer our Lord prayed just before His crucifixion. The prayer is filled with meaning for every believer, for in it Jesus prayed for us: "... those who will believe in me through their [the disciples'] message" (v. 20).

Jesus often called His disciples His "little children," and this is His prayer for their faithfulness and safety when He was no longer with them. If a mother were to paraphrase this prayer and pray it for her children, her prayer would be something like this:

Dear Lord,

I have told my children all about You, these children You gave me; they were Yours and You gave them to me, and they have kept Your Word.

My children know that everything I have is from You.

For everything You have revealed to me, I have given to them; they have received Your truth and believed it.

I pray for them, for these You have given me, for they are Yours.

They are in the world, and I come to You, Holy Father, and ask You to keep them true to Your name.

While they were under my authority, I kept them in Your name, and none of them perished.

But now I come to You, asking that they might know the fullness of joy.

I have given them Your Word; and the world has hated them, because they are not of the world, even as every Christian is not of the world.

I do not ask You to take them out of the world, but to keep them from the evil one.

They are not of the world, even as I am not of the world.

Sanctify them in the truth; Your Word is truth.

As You have sent me into the world, I send them into the world.

For their sakes I have sought to sanctify myself, so that they might be sanctified in truth.

I do not pray for my children alone, but for those also who will believe in You because of their faithful witness;

That we may all be one in You, You in us and us in You; that the world may believe that You love everyone, just as You loved us.

—John 17:6-23, Paraphrased

If the day comes when we can truthfully pray this prayer, we will have accomplished our purpose as mothers.

15

SUGGESTIONS FOR GROUP USE

Choose a meeting place suitable to the type and size of group you will have. This can be a Sunday school classroom or home, structured or informal. If the group is to meet in a home, it might be best to find one other than that of the leader. It is hard to turn people out of your own home when class is over, but the leader can encourage class members to leave on time by leaving someone else's home herself. It is easier to secure a hostess for any group if she knows people will leave promptly.

Set a time schedule for class sessions and stick to it faithfully. If coffee or other refreshments are served (this is not a necessity), include this in the schedule, but be sure that the lesson period *starts and ends on time*. It is the responsibility of the leader to keep faith with class members in the matter of time.

Approach each phase of the project prayerfully. Pray that God will guide your decisions, bring the right women to the classes, give you wisdom as you study the material, give you a love for each woman, and open each heart to His truth.

The leader may want to open each session with a presentation emphasizing material from the book or drawn from other sources (current newspaper and magazine articles or other books) before beginning the discussion time. During discussion the leader should keep things moving so that all questions are covered by the end of the allotted time. Scripture references not written out in the text should be looked up by group members and read aloud. Quiet women should be drawn into the discussion whenever possible so that more talkative women do not overpower them. The leader should discourage negativism and keep women thinking positively about their children and God's ability to meet their needs.

The "Before you read on" questions are designed to involve the reader personally in the material being presented and may not all be appropriate for group discussion. If the leader would like to use some of these in addition to the chapter-by-chapter questions, she should choose questions that will not embarrass members, or ask, "Which of these questions were the most interesting or thought-provoking for you?''

Each class session should be closed with an opportunity for class members to commit some area of their lives to the Lord. If they would like to share with the group what that commitment is, they should be given an opportunity to solidify their decision by doing so, but no one should feel pressured to make a public statement. The leader may use questions such as the following:

- Has this lesson revealed a specific area in your life which needs attention?
- Is the Lord prodding you to take some particular action with regard to a child or someone else in your life?
- Are you willing to make the changes, with God's help, that you feel He is impressing upon you?

The leader should then close in a prayer of dedication.

Getting the Group Started

This book can be used by individuals or in group situations, taking either fifteen, twelve, or eight sessions. If the group is to meet twelve or fifteen times, the leader should plan on taking forty-five minutes to one hour to cover each week's material. On the twelve-week schedule, chapters 1 and 2 should be combined into a single session, as should chapters 4 and 5. In order to cover the material in eight weeks, one and a half hours should be allotted each week. The first three chapters should be covered during the initial session, and approximately one and a half chapters thereafter.

If you choose the fifteen-week schedule, the first session will be spent in getting acquainted, passing out materials, etc. Otherwise, at the first session the leader should set aside fifteen or twenty minutes for group members to tell their names and the ages of their children. It is helpful to all, and especially the leader, to know the age range of the children represented—whether they are all preschoolers or if some will be asking questions with adolescents in mind as well. Name tags are helpful, especially if they are left with the leader each week so they can be worn during all the meetings.

At the first session, in as friendly and nonthreatening a manner as possible, the leader should set a few ground rules. These might include:

1. We will keep to our schedule, starting and ending on time.

2. Class members are asked to commit themselves to being prepared for each session, answering the "Before you read on" and "Making it personal" questions and studying thoroughly the assigned pages.

3. During discussions, unless the question calls for our personal opinion, we will avoid statements that start with "I think" or "I feel." Instead we will try to share what God is saying in the Bible.

4. We probably will not be able to solve individual family problems during class time. If class members have specific problems they wish to discuss with the leader, we encourage them to do it privately. (Nothing will drive people away quicker than to have group time monopolized by one or two individuals with many problems.)

5. Some of the questions that arise may be dealt with later in the book. If so, the leader will suggest the subject be postponed until reached in the material. (The leader must be thoroughly familiar with the contents of the book before classes start so she can guide discussions, and also so she will know how many weeks it will take for her group to cover the material.)

6. Family matters shared either purposefully or inadvertantly should not be discussed outside the group.

7. Class members are encouraged to pray for one another and for the leader.

The questions for discussion are suggestions only. The leader will want to be sure that topics she feels are of primary importance to her group are brought up for discussion and will want to add other questions to meet this need.

NOTES

Chapter 1

[1]Gloria Steinem, *Redbook*, January 1972.
[2]Ibid.
[3]Betty Friedan, Humanist Manifesto II, quoted in "Concerned Women for America" newsletter, P.O. Box 82957, San Diego, CA, 92138, 1980.
[4]Shirley MacLaine, *Redbook*, January 1972.
[5]Mary Jo Bane, quoted in "Concerned Women for America" newsletter, P.O. Box 82957, San Diego, CA, 92138, 1980.
[6]Candace Bergen, *Los Angeles Times*, 24 July 1977.

Chapter 8

[1]Fitzhugh Dodson, *How to Parent* (New York: Nash Publishing, 1970).

Chapter 11

[1]Saul Brown, *Los Angeles Times*, 17 January 1979.
[2]Daniel Durso, *American Home*, January 1977.

Chapter 12

[1]Mr. Rogers, *Mr. Roger's Neighborhood*, Public Broadcasting System.